FINDERS KEEPERS LOSERS WEEPERS

The Relationship Manual

Dr. Deena Moustafa, PhD

Bellissima Publishing, LLC
Jamul, California

www.bellissimapublishing.com

Copyright © 2011 by Bellissima Publishing, LLC

All rights reserved. No part of this book may be reproduced or transmitted in any form or by any means, electronic or mechanical, including any photocopying, or recording, or by any information or storage retrieval system, without permission from the publisher and author.

IBSN 978-1-935630-47-0
First Edition

Love is a many splendored Thing. . .

Finders Keepers Losers Weepers

The Relationship Manual

Dr. Deena Moustafa, PhD

1

Finders Keepers Losers Weepers

Preface

As we mature and we form romantic relationships, initially we may want to keep things light and uncomplicated. But as relationships deepen, most individuals feel an innate need to love and be loved in return. Before we get married we may be confused and ask is that my one and only? And after we get married we are working just to make sure our marriage works. Some on us have success. Others fail.

In the early days of romance you may often wonder how serious your partner is about you. But even those in serious relationships, whether living together or married, are not exempt from doubts. Just because he's told you at some point that he loves you or cares for you, this is no guarantee his feelings won't change. We need constant reassurance the loving feeling is still there.

As Goethe said "Love is an ideal thing, but marriage is a real thing." Love can be a noun and it can be a verb, Love is the answer for all our unanswered questions, Love is a life giving us the true meaning of life. Love is God's gift, Love is the way of giving us the map to the right ways in life. Love is the keyword of our happiness. And I think "Would you Marry me" is the best translation for "I love you," as "The most important thing a father can do for his children is to love their mother. This book is a book of thoughts; some of them are my thoughts and some of them belong to other people who have already lived their thoughts. It is coming with new ideas for a better life, ideas about how to have a relationship, how to live in a relationship, and how to face anything coming up your relationship, as well as how to live your life before and after marriage, how to get your one and only, how to treat your husband, how to treat your wife, and what you can do if you discover your spouse is cheating on you, what to do in an abusive relationship! (If you don't have a happy marriage at least have a happy divorce.) This book also tells you how to live your life after breakup, what do if you have had a rape experience; that is, what you must do and how to cope your feelings, and much, much more.

CHAPTER ONE

Love is not something that happens to you, but something that you MAKE happen to you.

Love is an action that if you don't use it, you lose it. Love is like any communication, GIVE and TAKE. If you didn't give, you cannot take. Love is something that grows from your actions and decisions. Whether you should get married is a very important decision. It should also be a very firm decision. You should stick by it because you made that decision. If there are worldly reasons for your loving someone, those reasons can one day go away. One day you may meet another person who has those qualities, things, or even feelings for you more than this person you think you love today. As you grow and change as a person, and as your position in life and in society changes, your likes and dislikes change. What you were satisfied with once, may not satisfy you anymore. You may even get bored with someone.

Keep expectations realistic. No one can be everything we might want him or her to be. Sometimes people disappoint us. It's not all-or-nothing, though. Healthy relationships mean accepting people as they are and not trying to change them!

Be flexible. Most of us try to keep people and situations just the way we like them to be. It's natural to feel apprehensive, even sad or angry when people or things change and we're not ready for it. Healthy relationships means change and growth are allowed!

Take care of you. You probably hope those around you like you, so you may try to please them. Don't forget to please yourself. Healthy relationships are mutual relationships!

Be dependable. If you make plans with someone, follow through with those plans. If you have an assignment deadline, meet it. If you take on a responsibility, complete it. Healthy relationships are trustworthy relationships!

Say, "I'm sorry" when you're wrong. It goes a long way in making things right again. Healthy relationships can admit mistakes.

Don't assume things. When we feel close to someone it's easy to think we know how he or she thinks and feels. We can be very wrong! Healthy relationships check things out.

Don't hold grudges. You don't have to accept anything and everything, but don't hold grudges—they just drain your energy. Studies show that the more we see the best in others, the better healthy relationships get. Healthy relationships don't hold on to past hurts and misunderstandings.

The goal is for everyone to be a winner. Relationships with winners and losers don't last. Healthy relationships are relationships between winners who seek answers to problems together.

Why We Get Married

For love:

Contrary to the pessimistic idea that marriage signals the end of romance, it marks the beginning of a whole new phase of being in love. Marriage allows lovers to enter into a partnership where two halves come together to form a stronger whole and where love evolves into a deeper, more committed relationship. If you really love your partner, marriage is one very powerful way of showing your partner in love that your commitment is for real, and invites them to feel and do the same.

For back-up:

Anyone living in a marriage of several years, knows how easily we take our partner's support for granted, such as when we fall ill, have an emergency at work or need to get the dessert with-the-Smiths-coming-over-in-an-hour-and-me-being-stuck-in-the-traffic.

For your health:

All jokes about grey hair and stress aside, men who are married live an average of 10 years longer than those who are not married. Not only that, but their quality of life and health go up as well. Sociologist Linda Waite's research shows men who are married engage in fewer risky behaviors, like excessive drinking or dangerous hobbies and careers. Married men also eat more healthily and see the doctor more often.

For happiness:

Even though so many men are choosing to marry later and later in life, often in their mid-30's or early 40's, these men are unhappy. Dr. Kimmel's work across the last three decades has shown that men are higher achieving when they are married. It's easy to be healthy when you're healthy, have a high income, and experience a high degree of sexual satisfaction.

For your finances:

A single residence, shared health insurance and other benefits, insurance breaks, and automatic inheritance rights give married couples big legal advantages when it comes to money. Married couples tend to have higher incomes than single couples.

For sex:

Married couples have sex more often, and report a higher rate of sexual satisfaction, according to the National Marriage Project. This applies even as couples get older, into their mid-40's and early 50's. This is a result of a number of factors including an evolving sense of trust, the absence of guilt for religious couples, security in the relationship, security in physical needs being met, a deeper understanding of what partners like and also proximity.

For raising a family:

Coping with various challenges that confront a family gives partners the chance and experience to grow as responsible members of society. Sociologists regard the family as the basic unit of the larger society, and thus it is no wonder that the best community leaders often emerge from the happiest of marriages.

Human society, since the beginning of its evolution, has been trying out various combinations of relationships; and the one paradigm that has stood the test of time is the heterosexual, monogamous relationship, most widely seen in a marriage. The married couple forms the most stable environment for having kids and raising them in a world increasingly splintered by violence, drugs and breakdown of kinship ties.

CHAPTER TWO
Fear of marriage

It is completely normal to be afraid before getting married. Many people are afraid of committing to one person for the rest of their life. Some are afraid of the marriage ending in divorce due to the high divorce rate. Others are afraid because of the expectation of having children.

Marriage is a lifetime commitment between two souls deeply in love with each other. Although nobody dreams of being divorced and couples work hard in marriage, some still fail. Consequently, there are those who are afraid to get married. There are many possibilities behind their beliefs, but one thing is for sure, they do not want to be committed. Here are some of the reasons why I think some people prefer to stay single.

When you are married, you are not just sharing the same last name, you are share the same bank account, the same mortgage, the same credit score, the same house, the same pets, the same children, pretty much the same EVERYTHING. Have you lived together already? Some psychologists believe this is an important step that a couple should experience long before getting married. Living together helps you prepare for a future to come. You get to know good and bad habits, and you realize if you are willing to deal with those habits forever. Living together helps you to really understand your partner before making the bigger step of getting married. I could go on, but these are some of the most important factors to consider before a full-on commitment for the rest of your life. But again, like I said earlier, it is completely normal to be a little scared when it comes to getting married. It takes a strong AND EMOTIONALLY MATURE person to get married and to make it work. It also takes maturity to handle the stresses of married life and all the problems that comes with married life.

It is said that a man needs a long time to start a relationship, and that a woman needs a long time to end a relationship.

A Woman can start a relationship more easily than a man "in most cases;" but she takes a long time to let this relationship go. When a woman wants to end a relationship she always pushes her partner to make the decision for her.

When a Man loves a Woman, periodically, he pulls away before he gets closer. Most people have two bottom-line fears when it comes to relationships: the fear of rejection, and the fear of engulfment, which means the fear of losing the other or the fear of losing yourself. These are deep fears that start in childhood and may continue throughout your life, making it difficult for you to be fully emotionally available in a relationship. These fears do not just go away. Until you develop a powerful, loving adult self, you may take rejection personally and not know how to handle loss. Without a strong loving inner adult, you may allow others to control you, giving yourself up to prevent rejection.

Again, these fears do not need to be healed before starting a relationship, but unless you are in the process of healing them and continue to do healing work within the relationship, there is a good chance that you will recreate another unsuccessful relationship.

A relationship is a wonderful arena for healing and growth when both people are devoted to learning to be strong loving adults. If you are on a devoted healing and learning path, make sure that your partner is there with you.

Marriage is about sharing, not completing.

Every time I hear someone say they feel another person completes them, I cannot stop thinking how incorrect they are. Marriage is not about completing each other; because God creates us as a complete person. When God created us, he created man as he created woman. We have the same duties and rights in front of God, and no one is above anyone, or completing anyone. When we get married, we look for someone to share our life.

The first social skill we learn as a young child is sharing. Since kindergarten, I can remember being told by my mother to share my lunch if someone didn't have food, to share my feelings with her, to share my toys with my friends, and so on and so forth. Through life we all learn how to share everything we have, feelings, money, space, vacations, hobbies. . . etc., with others.

Sharing in marriage encompasses every single aspect of sharing. We share feelings, our stuff, our money, our space, our lives. You need to change the way you talk about "your" stuff and make it "our" stuff, because you have committed your life to your spouse, everything that belongs to you also belongs to your spouse. You no longer belong just to yourself. And all of your decisions affect much more than just you when you are married.

Chapter Three

To catch a man is an art! To hold onto a man is a real job!

Keep in mind that "being married" is just a label, like "dating", or "girlfriend." So when you figure out you really want to be married, also make it clear to yourself what being married means to you. You need to be clear on what you expect from a spouse, so that when you say "Yes!" it means what you think it means.

A woman must have a strategy to get her man. If you want to win his heart and get the ring do not do these things:

No not cater to his every need: There's a great chance that if you do this – cater to every whim of a man – he's going to stick around, but it's not because you are the woman for him, it's because you'll do *anything* he wants. NEVER cook a man dinner every night. NEVER do his laundry if you are dating. NEVER clean his apartment for him, and NEVER run over to his place simply because he's feeling frisky.

Do not change your appearance for him: If you wear pink lipstick and the man you are dating says he prefers red, don't convert. If you do you are showing him that you are easily manipulated. Men like a woman with her own mind. Don't change who you are just because there's something about you he doesn't automatically like.

Do not act like his mother: Don't treat any man you are dating like a child. This means do not call him all the time. Don't ask him where he's been if you haven't heard from him in a while, and never tell him to button up his coat if it's cold outside. He already has a mother. He doesn't want you to be one too.

Do not assume he knows what you want: Men can't read minds. Their minds also don't operate the same way yours does. If you expect a man to know what you want from him, you'll always be disappointed.

Femininity is what makes women more attractive, not physical beauty and looks.

Not every pretty woman is feminine. Femininity is more of an attitude, style, behavior, personality, body language, not only body shape and looks. It is not your features and your body that make you feminine. It is a lot more than this. You don't have to be a beautiful woman to win a man's love. Trust me, I know, because I've talked to hundreds of men about this very thing. All that advice is wrong, wrong, wrong.

Since the earliest days of mankind, a woman has been able to show a man she is interested in him. The smart ones have always let the man think *he* is doing the chasing. This is the twenty first century, and you *can* show a man you are interested in him. Catch his eye, and then immediately look away, but then look back at him. If he finds you attractive, he will think he has found you, and he will most often make a move.

A changeable woman is attractive.

When a man feels or knows he owns your heart, you actually become less appealing to him. This seems backwards, but it's unfortunately true. In the dating stages of a relationship the man is all about the thrill of the chase. He wants nothing more than to pursue you so he can catch you. If you're the first to proclaim your undying love and devotion to him, his interest in you will wane. If you've already said the three little words to him, don't panic. This is a mistake that's easily undone.

You need to become less available and less accessible to him. Close your heart up a bit. Stop sending him soppy text messages and/or emails. Don't call him dozens of times during the day anymore. Let him start to do the work to win your heart. He will, because his interest will be recharged once he feels you're losing interest in him.

Changing is a really important thing. Inside changing will improve your relationship, and make your spouse or significant other more attached to you, more than outside changing. A woman told me once, "I hadn't changed my hair, my make-up or my clothes. I hadn't lost weight. Nothing had changed on the outside. But I could tell that I was changing on the inside. I realized this thing I'd discovered called 'feminine grace' was helping me use certain secrets to my benefit. My husband kept saying, 'I've never met a woman like you before,' and yet it was still me."

Remember, a successful relationship depends on two things:

(1) Finding the right person
(2) Being the right person

Write list of what you really want in your future husband. This list will help you determine what you are looking for, so that you spend a minimum amount of time pursuing the *wrong* people. It lets you determine quickly *who* to ask and *what* to ask. No matter how much is his bank balance, no matter he looks like, the important thing is he is just *Mr. Right*. Don't look for the perfect guy because there is no perfect guy on this earth; so my advice is if you find a 60-70% perfect guy, that should be enough.

CHAPTER FOUR

Good Communication = Good Marriage

If we want something, we need to say it.

Don't rely on your intuition. Ask. Some people have a very difficult time spelling out what they want from their spouses. "I shouldn't *have* to ask," they insist. "You should know on your own what I want. If I have to ask, then I would rather not have it!" This approach to life is childish and ineffective. Individuals express caring and develop love in different ways and at varying rates. Express yourself in a way that shows understanding of your spouse's personality, and your spouse will respond in kind.

Perhaps the most essential quality for good communication in any relationship, and particularly in a marriage, is to be a good listener.

Use "I" statements to express your feelings.

Don't use "you" statements, such as "You are!," "You never!," or, "You always!" Whenever you need to have a serious discussion with anyone, it is always advisable to begin with something positive.

You must be sincere and not use artificial praise as a form of manipulation.

Explain it and make me understand.

People often mistakenly assume that their feelings are universal. They think, "Anyone would feel the way I did." It is so obvious to them that their feelings were "normal" that they see no need to explain to their spouses exactly why they feel the way they do. Instead, they simply recount the disturbing events and let the tale speak for itself.

This is a serious mistake. If you do not explain, in the most specific language possible, exactly how you feel and felt, your spouse will not understand what bothered you or what is bothering you.

Don't say one thing and then act another way.

You can't expect your spouse to read your mind. Like the man who asked his wife who'd been giving him the silent treatment.

"Are you mad at me?" he asked
"I'm not mad," she replied.
"Are you sure nothing is wrong?" he asked.
"Nothing IS WRONG," she said.
So he tried one last time and said, "I can tell something is wrong."
To which she replied, "WELL, IF YOU DON'T KNOW WHAT IT IS, I'M NOT GOING TO TELL YOU."

Mixed messages and the silent treatment won't accomplish *anything* but problems.

Say what you like *before* what you don't like.

Don't hesitate to tell each other what you like. Too often married couples only say what they *don't* like. This can cause hurt feelings and make it seem like a hopeless situation. If you talk about the things that you enjoy and agree on, as much or more than the things you don't like or agree on, it creates a positive atmosphere in which to communicate.

Change yourself rather than your spouse.

When you notice things about your spouse that you would like to see change, remember that there are things about you that he would like to see change too. If you work on changing yourself, rather than on changing your spouse, you will see big changes in your perspective. Just do not give up who you are for your spouse. How you screw on the toothpaste cap is another matter altogether.

Find something to do together.

Look for an activity to do together. I did that with my fiancée.. First, I helped him in his work. I just gave this one hour daily. Then we did something for fun. We shared all about each other in a facebook group, and it helped *me* in my work! You cannot believe what happened!! Now we have a lot of friends in common. I know a lot of things about his work, so if has problem he can communicate with me; and we are look to find a solutions together. It is really cool!

Marriage is two persons looking in the same direction.

It is not necessary for two people to see things exactly alike. Make it easy for your spouse to begin talking by being willing and making it clear that you are in this together. When both of you are working toward the same goal - a happy, healthy, lifelong marriage - being available to one another *has* to come first.

Don't argue! Agree to disagree.

You don't agree on everything. So what? Opinion is a personal thing that does not make or break a relationship. Allow differences of opinion, and accept that your opinion may not be the only opinion that is right.

Stop blaming your spouse.

When you blame your spouse, you are acting as though they are beneath you and not an equal partner. You are implying that you are smarter than they are and are thus more powerful. To have a healthy marriage, both partners must feel as if they are equals, and that both share equally in strength.

Love is the most lasting bond of union.

You and your spouse will have your hearts bound together in lasting love. This is by far the most important reason why you need to have good communication in your marriage.

Become best friends with your spouse.

While your husband might not notice it when you change your hairstyle or wear a new outfit, there is one thing he will notice for certain. When you treat him as a dear friend--as well as your romantic lover--he feels important, special, heard and loved. Men are drawn and highly attracted to women who make them feel this way. By becoming your husband's best friend, your marriage will be even stronger and sexier than it was. Finally, remember you don't want to communicate to someone but WITH someone.

CHAPTER FIVE

Love is not blind. Love has a sharp vision.

Love is *not* blind. It has a great vision. We just put obstacles in the way, such as my partner will change, my partner doesn't mean to hurt me, etc.. You must take off those rock glasses and see your partner as he or she is. For example, when a man truly loves you, he will honor and respect you. If he doesn't, do not deceive yourself and do not allow him to defraud you. He DOES NOT love OR care about you! Don't say he will change after marriage. Angry, bitter, hostile, combative, unforgiving single women, become angry, bitter, hostile and combative, unforgiving wives. They will *never* change! All you need to do is to follow this advice. Think with your *mind* and *feel* with your heart.

He said "I love you."
She replied "I love you too."

BUT *both of them loved each other in their own way.*

Men and women are as different psychologically as they are physically. The psychological differences between men and women are less obvious. They can be difficult to describe. Yet these differences can profoundly influence how we form and maintain relationships that can range from work and friendships to marriage and parenting. People in relationships often have strong expectations that their partner will be just like they are, exhibit the same attitudes, values, perceptions and behaviors. So it is very important to educate yourself as to the basic gender differences that exist between men and women, and accept the that differences are there. They are real, and they are not going away. In this way, you can learn to use the differences to *enrich* your relationship, rather than to damage it.

What is a relationship, and what happens when it ends?

First of all, a man does not call a relationship a relationship. When a relationship ends, a woman will cry and pour her heart out to her girlfriends, and she will write a poem on facebook and invite her friends to comment. Then she will get on with her life. A man has a little more trouble letting go.

Women understand with words and emotion.

Men believe if women appear satisfied, that's sufficient. They think women already know how they feel, so why should they have to remind them how much they love them? Women want men to *say* words of endearment.

Because of our lack of ability to allow our emotions to affect us, men have labeled women as unreasonable, difficult to understand and hard to please. Women are born less rational and more emotional than men, which makes women susceptible to environmental conditions and perception of situations and also to the emotions we experience.

Women tend to find their identity in close relationships, while men gain their identity through vocations.

Because a woman's emotional identity is with people and places around her, she needs more time to adjust to change that may affect her relationships. A man can logically deduce the benefits of a change and get "psyched-up" for it in a matter of minutes. It is not so with a woman. Since she focuses on the immediate consequences of things, of relocating, for example, she needs time to overcome the initial adjustment before warming up to the advantages of it. Men tend to express their hostility through physical violence, while women tend to be more verbally expressive.

Men, Women and Sex

Women's sexual inclinations are more complicated than men's. What turns women on sexually? Women do not always know. Men get aroused by different things than those things that arouse a woman. Sexual desire in women is extremely sensitive to environment and context. A woman's sexual drive tends to be related to her menstrual cycle, while a man's drive is fairly constant. The hormone testosterone is a major factor in stimulating a man's sexual desire.

Many believe men want sex more often than women at the start of a relationship, in the middle of it, and after many years of it. It is widely held that men want to connect with the physical act, because the act of release during sex is how a man most feels connected. It is the "feeling of being connected" men seek.

Women and men view the role of sex differently. Women want to talk, connect, and then have sex. For men, sex is the connection. Sex is the language men use to express their tender loving vulnerable side. Sex is for men, the language of intimacy.

While a man needs little or no preparation for sex, a woman often needs hours of emotional and mental preparation. Harsh or abusive treatment can easily remove her desire for sexual intimacy for days at a time. Men are more likely to seek sex even when it is frowned upon or even outlawed.

Men, Women, And Unselfish Love

Men enter marriage knowing everything about sex and very little about genuine, unselfish love. I am not saying men are more selfish than women. I'm simply saying that at the outset of a marriage, a man is not as equipped to express unselfish love or as desirous of nurturing marriage into a loving and lasting relationship as a woman is.

Men tend to focus on one problem at a time or a limited number of problems at a time, while women tend to be intuitive global thinkers.

A male may work through a problem repeatedly, talking about the same thing over and over, rather than trying to address the problem all at once. Women are prone to become overwhelmed with complexities that "exist," or may exist, and may have difficulty separating their personal experience from problems.

A man's thinking tends to be concrete, while a woman's thinking tends to be abstract.

When I say that I mean man tend to describe and talking about love literalness and the tendency to be bound to the most immediate and obvious sense impressions, "when I hug you I feel love" or "kiss me to feel you are in love with me" he needs something Tangible to talk about love, on the contrary, woman talking about love as emotions, she uses concepts to talk about love "when I loved you I feel like I own this world!"

How do men and women share problems?

A Woman shares her problems when she has one, the first thing she think about it is to pick up her phone and call her close friends to talk about her problem; Women know that there's no one like a good girl friend to talk to when you've had a bad day, this way makes her feel good, on the contrary, man prefers to keep his problem inside, he go to his room or lying on sofa and watching news

Finders Keepers Losers Weepers

When a woman shares her problems with a man, she is not looking for solutions – she needs someone to listen to her, on the contrary, man shares a problem – if he does that- looking for some solutions.

What shall we do and where shall we go?

For most women it doesn't matter where they go or what they do. The target of going out is to TALK, they talk about everything and everyone, people, family, shopping, work, etc.. On the other hand, men relate to their friends by doing things together such as fishing, watching and/or playing football, and even when they talking about women they do *that* while they are doing something else.

We are different, but we still can make it.

Men and women are different. When they are in relationship they come together, but there are, in effect, two worlds—his and hers. They have different values, priorities, and habits. They play by different rules, her rules and his rules! But still, there are situations that must be conducted by THEIR rules.

1. The woman says, "You don't love me anymore" man replies "Then why am I still here with you?" (This is the wrong answer) The woman doesn't want to hear this. She just wants a hug and for him to say, "Sure, I love you." A man must not think or assume because he is in a relationship with a woman and because he has not run-off, the woman will automatically know and be assured he still loves her.

2. When woman has a bad day, she needs someone to listen to her. Don't give her a solution. Just listen to her.

3. Study your partner well. What works with one woman doesn't work with another. Some men don't understand the concept of this in verbal communication. They just don't get the message. If you are a woman and you've tried to talk to your partner,

and it doesn't work, you must be silent for a while. Then he will try to figure out *why* you aren't talking to him.

4. Choose the right time to make love. Many women feel like prostitutes when they're forced to make love when they are feeling resentment toward their husbands. However, a man may have NO idea what he is putting his wife through when he forces sex upon her.

5. When you think you have 2 children to care for, you really have THREE children to care for, because the third is your husband. Someday your two children will leave home. Your husband will live with you until the last day of your life.

6. When woman says she needs a break, she wants you to take care of her.

7. Do not try to calm down an angry woman. Women are born less rational and more emotional than men.

8. When entering a room, men look for exits, estimating a possible threat, and ways of escape, while women pay attention to the guests' faces to find out who they are and how they feel.

9. The only way to understand a woman is to love her - and then it isn't necessary to understand her. To women, love is an occupation. To men, it is a preoccupation. To be happy with a man you must understand him a lot and love him a little. To be happy with a woman, you must love her a lot and not try to understand her at all.

10. Don't expect to understand a woman's reactions. I have been a woman for 32 years, and I am still shocked by my own reactions.

11. No one will change. The effort you make to change someone is a waste of time. Don't ever delude yourself! Your beauty, fine body, sexual prowess, cooking skills, femininity and vibrant personality will never be enough to change a man, NEVER! And if it is, he isn't a man at all.

Chapter Six

Marriage is a dialogue, not a monologue.
A dialogue means listening and understanding, not proving and convincing.

Listen:

When your partner wants to talk to you, it is important to stop what you are doing to listen. It is not good to halfway listen. Sincerely make time for one another.

Talk:

Please talk to your partner about *all* the issues that matter to you. Talk to your partner about your feelings and your expectations. That will help cement a better relationship, because your partner will know what you believe is needed to make the relationship stronger.

Choose a good time for serious conversation:

If there is something on your mind, think about the subject that you plan to talk about in advance. Talking may not be the problem, but timing can be everything. This is especially important for serious conversations.

Respect differences:

"My husband just can't communicate." "I just can't get a straight answer from my wife."

There is no arguing that men and women communicate differently. God wired-up men and women *very* differently. While women focus on talking, men focus on fixing things and finding solutions. Once you understand how the other person sees things, it is much easier to avoid problems.

Clear your mind, and think before you speak. Men, remember that men and women communicate in very different ways, and that your wife may not hear what you are trying to say if you just blurt it out in man-speak. Keep her point of view in mind.

Discuss:

If you do not discuss problems in relationships and marriage, they can fester and grow and eventually destroy the relationship altogether. Communication is essential. **But** remember to discuss things in a calm, kind manner. Pick a time and place without distraction. You and he need each other's full attention and respect during this time. If you discuss things gently and kindly, and are respectful of your partner's feelings, then this will go a long way in resolving your communication problems.

Accept your partner as he or she is:

You can generally expect the same. When you communicate with your partner, be sure to let him/her know that you accept his or her feelings and that you love him or her.

Be physical:

The good morning kiss, the hug before you leave for work and return home, the small of the back touch when you walk by or want them to slide over---all these kinds of physical touch and more--- give your spouse the acknowledgement that you are there and you love them dearly.

Find new phraseology:

Delete the words, "If you loved me you would. . ." and replace them with, "I feel loved when you. . ." This brings your feelings out into the open where your husband can understand them. Don't use terms such as "you always" and "I never."

Assume nothing:

When your husband doesn't give you a hug when you come home from work, you think you KNOW one hundred percent, beyond a shadow of a doubt that he doesn't love you like he should. This type of thinking blocks communication.

Excuse:

You are anticipating a romantic evening. But your husband comes home late from work. While you were waiting, you found your emotions changing and you are now feeling lonely, unwanted and VERY IRRITATED! However, it doesn't mean that he *intended* to make you feel that way. So try to find a list of excuses for him not just one excuse. He may not have realized or understood how important the anniversary was to you, as many men do not place priority on the same things women do. Or it is possible that he was on his way home and something out of his control changed his destination or time frame causing him to be late. There are many reasons why he could have been late.

Be patient:

People forget things and make mistakes. Look beyond the obvious to the true motive behind the action. Each spouse can have a different personality, a different background, and bring a different approach to problems. This can come with different role models, separate experiences, and different values growing up into adulthood.

Forgive and forget:

Don't rehash the past. If something is in the past, has already been dealt with and resolved, leave it there. Bringing up the past is a communication killer.

Chapter Seven

He loves me. He loves me not.
Signs he loves you...

He makes you feel special.

He brings you flowers or wakes up extra early to bring you breakfast in bed. He's always going out of his way to make you feel exceptional. He is sending Early SMS just to tell you how much you are special.

Saying, 'I love you' and Showing 'I love you' are different things.

A lot of men assume that their women know they're loved and don't really tell them often enough. If he says those three words and says them often, count yourself lucky. Some men aren't exactly good with words and expressing their feelings. But they choose their own avenues of expression. This kind of guy does things, little or big, to show you how much you mean to him. That may include ordering take-away when he thinks you need a break from cooking or taking the kids off your hands so that you can have some time to yourself. Yes, you may need to hear the words from him, but actions sometimes speak louder than words.

He listens to you.

When you're talking, he's genuinely interested in what you're saying and gives you his undivided attention. He looks at you (not at the television blaring in the background or at the newspaper in his hand) and responds appropriately and gives you the feeling that he's really concerned about *your* concerns.

He takes care of you.

If he loves you he will give you a lot of care and affection. If something upsets you concerning his family or friends, he will try to see your side of it. He feels for you and even if he's seen you cry a thousand times before, he will still try to make you feel better and he will have that tissue box at hand. He will be happy when you are joyful and sad when you are down. A smile on your face will always make him smile. He does small and unexpected things that make you understand how much you mean to him. He's always careful to detail and knows what you like and what you do not like. You feel like you are his princess.

He calls you for no reason.

If he calls you more than twice in a day with nothing specific to say to you, there is a very good chance he is in love with you; because men would never do such a thing under ordinary circumstances. He can't control himself thinking of you for no apparent reason, and he wonders if you think of him half as much as he thinks of you.

His friends and family respect you

Sometimes you can gauge how a man feels about you from the way his circle of friends and close family behave around you. If they hold you in high regard, you can be sure he's been telling them just how happy he is to have you in his life.

He asks for your opinion.

When important decisions are at stake, either concerning him or both of you jointly or even the kids, he doesn't just go ahead and do what he thinks is right. He asks for your advice and not just for the sake of it. He often considers it and may even go by it. Or if he doesn't, he tells you why he didn't. and He helps you even if you don't ask for help and accepts you to help him. This way, you're a real team.

He shares almost all things with you.

What his is yours. There are some possessions men have that they would kill to protect from the grubby hands of the outside world; for example limited edition CDs, his car, his private notebook or football jerseys or caps. No one ever laid their fingers on these sacred items; and suddenly he asks that you take his CD home, or offers his threadbare shorts when you stay over, take this as a sign of his highest trust in you, and be very, very respectful of whatever it is he has decided to share.

He wants to spend more time with you:

He dedicates to you all his free moments, and you have great fun when you are together. He makes efforts to date you or to arrive to a show or event at which you insist to go. He never complains that he missed other things in order to be with you.

Eyes never lie.

You can see love in a person's eyes. The person in love with you has a special shine in his eyes when he's talking with you.

To test man's love call him at 4:00 a.m. to tell him how much you miss him and observe the reaction!

Or call him at 4 a.m. and tell him you are sick ~ if he comes over to take care of you, he is a keeper. Well, some people will find this funny, but it really works. It is very nice test. If he is really in love, he will answer and tell you how much he misses you, and that he saw you in his dreams. (You can also call him at 4.00 p.m. "while he is working" and tell him how much you miss him and observe his reaction.)

Women are more self-controlled when waking up from sleep, and wouldn't react similarly to men. I think women are more tolerant and would control themselves from either reacting or shouting back into the telephone so this isn't a good test for men to try on women.

Do you really know me or do you just think you do?

No matter how long you have been married, there are always some things you have yet to know about your spouse. These may have to do with his or her background, profession, personality or social life. While there is no guarantee that a couple who understand each other perfectly, will never go through a marital crisis, knowing your partner's dreams, values and expectations will definitely prepare you better for the journey that is marriage.

Most couples who have been married for quite some time begin to feel that they know everything that there is to know about the other person. But in reality, how much do you know about the person you wake up next to every morning? Details about family, work, personality and dreams of the future may remain unknown to even the most loving of spouses. Having a limited knowledge of your partner's past may not foretell a crisis in your marriage; but an awareness of likes and dislikes, ambitions and anxieties, may enable you to understand him or her better.

Knowing your spouse's family is a good step toward knowing your spouse.

Consider what you know about your spouse's family. While you may be able to reel off the names of your spouse's siblings, aunts and uncles, ask yourself if you are aware of spouse's ancestry. hat are the festivals fervently celebrated in their homes? On what occasions does the whole family gets together? Do you know which of the relatives your spouse likes least and the one he or she respects most? While members of your spouse's extended family may have little bearing on your marriage, remember that to know a person, you have to be aware of the influences and values that molded your spouse in the formative years of childhood.

You need to be his or her best friend.

Are you aware of your partner's deepest aspirations and his life-long dreams? Do you know what makes her most anxious or raises his hackles? Ask yourself if you both agree on the basic values and goals in life. While you may or may not agree with your spouse's religious and political convictions, do you know what they are? It helps to be aware of your partner's guiding philosophy in life, as well as his or her wider spectrum of values and ideals, in order to better know him or her as a person.

Share your dreams.

Do you know where your spouse wants to be professionally in another ten years? You may have met your spouse's boss and co-workers at office parties, but what about the dynamics of these relationships? Has your partner told you which colleagues have a way of making trouble and why the boss seems to be overlooking his recent achievements? In many cases, people prefer not to let office politics *infect* their home atmosphere and to a certain extent, they are justified in doing so. However, knowing the pulls and pressures your spouse faces at work *may* enable you to better understand fluctuations in his or her moods and raise the level of your respect for your partner as a professional.

Sex to marriage is like gas to a car.

A car cannot move without gas and gas is nothing without a car. Sex is generally a hurried affair, to be finished before one crashes for the night. So, if you want to know your spouse as a lover, ask him what he or she would like to do tonight and how to do it. Get to know what turns your spouse on - a sensuous massage, romantic music or racy lingerie are some choices. Share your sexual fantasies, or take a shower together. While sex is not *everything* or even the most *important* part of marriage, it is a strong indicator of the health of the marriage.

Knowing your spouse is more than living with him.

Focus on your spouse's ways and habits around the house – does he squeeze the toothpaste up from the bottom, or does she prefer cats to dogs as house pets? Is it important to your partner that the two of you eat dinner together, or is he freaked out at finding you have "arranged" his wardrobe? While these little quirks may seem mundane, they can often be significant pointers to the kind of person your spouse is.

CHAPTER EIGHT

Your Partner Is A Package!
Take your partner's deficits with his merits!

We are human, we have deficits and we have merits. We are not angels or devils. Sometimes what you see as a deficit, another person sees as a merit. You must take your partner as a package. Study yourself very well. Then study your partner and look at your partner's deficits another way. Can you coexist with them along with the merits?

Love your partner because of who they are. Don't love the idea of your partner. Do not think time will make your partner change, and you will wake up one day and find your Cinderella or your Prince Charming. Your partner is your Cinderella or Prince Charming because of who they are.

In a survey it was asked "Should you change the person you are to save a relationship? 27% agreed and 73% disagreed. Yes, one could change one of his or her flaws to save a relationship, as we always try to do with our family. We try to avoid things we do that could bother others. But there are some things about us that are unchangeable, such as the person we happen to be. Don't change the person you are. You need to be loved for the person you are, and you need to love others for the people they are.

Think with your heart and feel with your mind.

Divorce is increasing these days because a lot of people choose partners the wrong way. Some choose a partner just because they think they are in love, and they think the deficits they are seeing will disappear after marriage. All they think about is WE HAVE TO GET MARRIED no matter what, whether we are good for each other or not. And some people, because of their bad experiences, may choose partners by saying one plus one must equal two, or by saying "After marriage I will feel love." Marriage is not like that!

Love alone is not enough for having a good marriage, but there is never any guarantee of a good marriage, even if you think you have chosen carefully! You may ask, "What can I do to choose my spouse and have a good marriage?" The answer is you have to *"Think with your heart and feel with your mind,"* which means don't let *just* your heart lead you into marriage, because your marriage may based on lust more than love, and then your marriage will be too fragile. And don't let your mind lead you either. Your marriage will not have the warmth of love you need.

You must use both your heart and your mind. The best advice I have (if you are in doubt about your partner and are considering marriage) is to take a paper and pen and list everything about your partner, his merits and his deficits, and then give every point a percentage value. If the score is near 75%, go ahead and consider the marriage. If it is between 60% and 70%, give yourself time to reevaluate. If the score is less than 60%, get out. You deserve 100%. Keep in mind no one, not even you, is perfect.

Remember you are my husband, not my boss.
It is a marriage contract not a hiring contract.

Finders Keepers Losers Weepers

Neither partner should be the boss of the other. But for practicality one or the other may take the leadership in certain parts of their lives together (It can get very confusing and messy if both try to lead.) Neither party should be forced to do the other's bidding. In reality, though I think women tend to be the boss of the household and family, while the man plays the enforcer of her rules. We go through life together, hand in hand, not her behind him. With a wife as a partner instead of a subordinate, you have a better life, someone with whom you can share your life, not someone for whom you are responsible.

Some men misunderstand what God meant when He said 'man is the head of the family.' As such they want to stand on that and become the BOSS of the house instead of the lovely husband God wants them to be. Husband and wife should be equal. Make "all" choices together and talk about all things. It's not fair if a husband treats his wife like an employee, and just gives orders. You are, or become, what you allow yourself to be or become. There should be total equality in a marriage. If he is treating you like an employee, you are allowing him to do so. You can't control his behavior, but you can control how you respond to it.

Ask him if he has employees, and when he says yes, you say, "Be a boss to your employees NOT to me!" Then tell him, "When you marry someone, you spend a lifetime with that person. You don't spend a lifetime with an employee."

CHAPTER NINE

Contrary to popular belief, some men are attracted to a woman's personality.
"Beauty gets attention. Personality wins the heart."

Guys are "attracted" to the outside but they intuitively see what's inside right away. There is sexual attraction and there is attraction of the heart. It is important to realize there is a difference, because who a woman attracts, is in large part, based on what is attractive about her. Men fall in love a lot quicker with women who are more understanding about who they are why they do the things they do. If you lack the ability to understand the men you date, then you will most certainly not have a large pool of men from which to select. The more understanding and accepting you are of the man you are dating, the more he will love and accept you for who you are. The more adaptable you are to situations, the more men will like you. Be spontaneous. Men will be more attracted to you if they know that you can get up and go at anytime without much notice.

There is really no deep, dark secret to understanding men. Men are strongly influenced by their upbringing and their associations. If a woman wants to know the basic characteristics of a particular man, then she should get to know his friends. Guys hang around other guys like themselves.

Finders Keepers Losers Weepers

Many women fail to realize it is not nearly as important to understand all men as it is to understand that one man in their lives. Men come in all shapes, sizes, energy levels, and skin tones. But they are also products of different home environments, academic backgrounds, social influences, and past relationship experiences. All of these influences have had some impact on their thoughts, beliefs, and emotions, and largely determines how they approach or express themselves in subsequent relationships.

A clear personality is an attractive personality. Men do not like women who play games or never say what is on their minds. The more direct you are and the less a man has to guess about what is on your mind the better. Men are attracted to women who are intelligent. Men frequently end relationships with beautiful women because beauty is all they have.

An open-minded woman who doesn't take herself too seriously, and who can handle a harsh joke, and dish out one of her own will be much more attractive to men than the tightly wound woman who takes herself too seriously.

Just as important as things that you do or who you are, are things that you are NOT: not talking too much or too loudly, not being too aggressive or overly self-focused in your interaction with a man, not being overdressed, and not using too much make-up are just a few things that you can choose NOT to do and thus make yourself more attractive.

Another thing to remember is that it is impossible to separate physical attractiveness from personality. When a man looks at a woman he sees her mannerisms, the way she carries herself, her manner of speaking, her style decisions, the way she smiles or doesn't smile, etc. The brain can, in a split second, get a lot of information other than physical appearance.

Contrary to belief, a woman can understand a man's feelings, but not his way of thinking.

Men and women feel the same kind of emotions, and it is how they portray those emotions that make them different. Here is how you can understand your man's way of thinking.

1. Determine his personality type. In classic Myers-Briggs personality typing, roughly 60 percent of all men can be classified as "thinkers" (T-types), while about 60 percent of all women are "feelers" (F-types). This is one of most basic differences between the way men and women think. What this means is the most men make decisions based on what is reasonable, or logical. F-types prefer to make choices based on empathy, balance, harmony and what fits with personal values.
2. Men are considered logical and women are considered impulsive. Men think logically for a long period of time about falling in love or pursuing a relationship.
3. For women, it only takes tingles and goose bumps to know they are in love.
4. Deciphering how your man thinks is easy to do as long as you give it time to think about it.

You see, absolutely everything is different. Men think logically for a long time about falling in love while women just use tingles to tell them everything they need to know about love. A man's brain is easy to understand. It just requires more time, and the logic needs to be obvious.

Just because your partner isn't romantic, it doesn't mean he or she doesn't love you.

Finders Keepers Losers Weepers

I think everyone is romantic inside, but some can't express it or don't know how to express it! It doesn't mean the person doesn't love his or her partner. Just co-operate your partner and let your partner know how you want to be romanced, and you will get your feedback. It's like a style of expression. Romance is a way expressing love and his style can be different and unromantic for you, but probably the best way of romance for him. He wants to say and do what you want to hear and what you want him to do. It's like a radio transmission. It is always there, you just need to tune in yourself. Expressing love is important. A woman gets more confused about a relationship if she doesn't get romantic validation from her lover or husband. A poet once said that "A woman loves like a river and a man loves like a cascade;" but I believe both should balance.

Chapter Ten

How to Keep the Romance Alive in a Marriage

Express your love.

Saying "I love you" is the basic tenet of romance, but follow it up with a reason. Once a marriage becomes boring, you keep saying or doing things that you no longer mean. You may say "I love you" while leaving for work or before hanging up on the phone, out of mere habit. On the other hand, if you remind your partner why you love him or her, it will mean something special. For instance if you say, "I love you for the way you look to me" or "I love you because after ten years of marriage, you still laugh at my jokes," this will not only show your spouse that you still care, but that you love him or her as deeply as you always have.

Ask about one another.

After a few years of marriage, you might feel you already know everything there is to know about the other person and there can be nothing new. Yet, continue to inquire about your partner's day after he or she comes back from work. Ask how your spouse is feeling if your spouse appears upset. Start with simple questions that show you care and gradually widen your communication to include more important matters that your partner might want to share with you.

Make time for each other.

This must be the most common piece of advice given to couples, and yet the most difficult to follow. A busy household with kids, school work and domestic chores seems to sap away all your time and energy. Yet, spending even fifteen minutes with each other can make a huge difference. Make sure this time is for only the two of you – no discussing bills, sick kids or schedules for the next day. Wipe out every things-to-do list from your mind and focus only on each other. Tell a joke, hum a tune or simply massage his or her neck. Stick to such this ritual and see how it works wonders for your marriage.

Kiss each other for no apparent reason.

If you are doing this after a very long hiatus, you may initially feel foolish. Then remind yourself how things were before you got married. Did you need a reason to pucker up to your partner? I bet you didn't! Go back to the good times and rekindle the magic!

Indulge your partner.

This can be as simple as buying roses for your wife, or making your hubby's favorite dessert. Or you can put in some time and effort into your romantic gestures, like shopping for your wife's best perfume, or getting tickets for a game of your hubby's favorite football team. Whatever you do, it will remind your spouse that he or she is special to you, even after all the years of marriage.

Plan a regular night out

Most of us make the mistake of believing romance should be spontaneous, and if it is planned, somehow it is not the real thing. Leave such assumptions for teenagers, since you, as a long-married partner, know every kind of magic needs a bit of preparation and a lot of practice. Plan a "date" with your spouse and arrange a babysitter for the kids. Keep the evening free of interruptions from work and take pains to dress nicely. After a few nights of "dates" you will find the old warmth returning to your relationship.

Celebrate special occasions.

Always make it a point to observe special occasions. Remember anniversaries and significant days, like the time you found out that you were going to have your first child. Remember the first time you went on a date or kissed each other. It need not be an elaborate celebration, just remind yourselves of the many special memories you both share. It will work wonders for your marriage.

Romance means different things to different people.

Remember that romance means different things to different people. While you may crave candlelight dinners and soft music, your partner's idea of a romantic night out may be cozying up under a blanket of stars before a crackling campfire. Know and understand the other person's preferences and explore romantic ideas accordingly. If you are too rigid in your ideas of what is romantic and what is not, you might be letting yourself in for disappointments. Who knows? You may *even* find yourself liking something you *never* thought possible. After all, isn't this half the charm of marriage – discovering new things about yourself as you travel a new way with your partner?

So, if you feel your marriage hitting a plateau, where nothing interesting is happening anymore, take matters into your own hands. Rekindle the spark that first brought the two of you together and watch as the flames of romance once again bring the glow back into your marriage.

Being in a relationship doesn't mean you lose your freedom.

Finders Keepers Losers Weepers

How can you lose your freedom? Love is not jail. The more freedom you have, the more responsibilities you have to bear. Freedom in a relationship is when you and your other half feel you can be yourselves and not feel pressured to be anything else. Sometimes you lose this if your partner is possessive, but when there is mutual understanding, respect, communication, honesty and true love, you will *never* lose your freedom. You are free to do whatever you want to in your life, and you can discuss everything with your mate. But never use your freedom for doing bad things such lying or cheating. If you are honest about your wants and your needs your partner will respect them. If not, don't be in that kind of relationship.

Acceptance in a healthy relationship says, "People in my life, including those I'm closest to, are going to make blunders; and more than occasionally I will be angry, sad, depressed, or scared. I accept this as natural. I don't condone the mistakes of others, but I don't judge them either. Instead, I practice compassion and seek to understand them. I see emotion as part of the tapestry of life, something with which we all are learning to deal. I don't shy away from emotion. It's life. I'm also not a doormat. I practice dealing with the ups and downs of others as effectively as I can. I speak up about wrong-doing. I listen to frustrations about me with a willing ear, but I don't tolerate abuse."

Acceptance leads to freedom in a relationship, because one is no longer tied down by the bonds of expectation and demand. A person can still desire and hope for certain outcomes; but with acceptance, he frees himself from the result, whatever it may be. Acceptance is the gift of freedom to others and to oneself.

CHAPTER ELEVEN

A husband who does not respect his wife is not a man at all!

Respect can sometimes be an old-fashioned word. At times it can be downright annoying, because it seems to be the one ingredient that's been minced, sliced, grated and chopped many times over, especially in relationship and marriage manuals and how-to books. Respect begets respect. Respect in marriage is the key to fulfilling relationships and well-bred, considerate children. It may sound rather repetitious and stale, but when there's respect in a marriage, the integrity of marriage as an institution remains intact.

Respect is the value you place on the ability of your spouse to do something. This 'something' can be found in inter-personal relationships, managing the home finances, managing home and career, taking care of the kids, and the like. The value you place on your spouse's special abilities makes your spouse feel appreciated and loved. Respect means being truly interested in how the other person feels and thinks about a topic, and allows them to have their own set of values, beliefs, likes and dislikes. Respect means their opinion matters, even if you disagree with it. Respect means allowing the other person to live without being made to feel "less than" for the choices they make.

Everybody likes being treated with respect.

Imagine a home where each spouse contradicts the other, implying their counterparts have no idea what they are doing or saying. At every major decision they impresses upon one another that they have no confidence in the opinions of the other and that they do not thing anything good will come the position the other is taking. How long do you think a marriage like this will last?

If there is no respect, there is no love.

Sometimes love can be confused with respect. If you want to be with your true love forever, respect him. Give him his own space. Do not break into his privacy. Try to understand his point of view, even when you disagree. You may be very much in love and have strong emotions for him, but don't hold him back.

Respect, like communication, is a basic ingredient of a good marriage. It is a way of saying, "I know you can do this. I trust you." It is a feeling that promotes interdependency important in any relationship or marriage. Without interdependency a marriage is just two people living together. You have to need one another, and you have to enjoy having the other do things for you – not because you might not be able to do it yourself, but because you love your spouse doing it.

Respect matures into healthy companionship once sex and physical attraction lessens with age. If you do not respect your spouse's opinion, you can't communicate. Without communication, the marriage will collapse like a pricked balloon once the sexual attraction wanes.

Marriage is hard work.

Marriage is not hilariously happy all the time. Mutual respect, consideration and good manners will take a couple through those times when married life is not a bed of roses. Respect is one of the foundations on which a good marriage is built. Small, kind, loving acts showed between one another always gains deep respect. It sends silent messages of "You are important to me. . ." and "You really do love me."

To make a marriage successful, mutual respect is the keyword.

When you respect your partner's view, you get the same vibes in return; and this makes the relationship grow stronger. However, marriage is not *only* about two people being together. Most married couples with kids would agree that a hostile atmosphere at home adds to the deterioration of the mental and physical health of any kids or elderly in the home. Have you ever seen happy, well adjusted children in a family where the husband and wife are always at odds? You need to sort out your issues in a more mature way, so that you can lead your children by example. With a growing number of stress related problems, married couples also need to create a respectful environment for their health as well. Simply put, in order to be happy, learn to let go.

Respect is one of the most important things you can give to your children.

Some parents take a child's side against the other spouse. This is not only disrespectful to the spouse, but it also gives the child the idea he or she can drive a wedge between the parents and get their own way. The end result is the child feels insecure. If, for example, your husband or wife has forbidden the child something, and you disagree with what your spouse has said, you need to take this up with your spouse at a time when the child is not present and is out of earshot. Parents should always present a united front to their children.

Only mutual respect between humans can bring them closer:

Married people who respect each other do not look outside the marriage arrangement to solve problems. They do not discuss problems inside the marriage with a third outside party, best friend or confidante. This cheapens the marriage and creates anger in the other spouse. Marriage and all that goes with it belongs between two loving, mature individuals.

Chapter Twelve

When you decide to play, please stay away from hearts! Hearts are not Toys!

The heart is precious. Do not play games with it. Both genders are guilty of this, and both genders play with hearts, but for different reasons. For men may be covering a sensitive, insecure self by portraying the confident, conquering male, saying and doing whatever it takes to convince a woman to be with him. If you've even remotely experienced the dating scene, you know men play games. These games tend to frustrate women and make them try even harder to secure the attention of the man. In the end this turns the man off, and he ends up leavng.

Games are often about boosting a man's ego.

Realize he wants be the "man." Games are often about boosting a man's ego. If a guy waits to call you, he feels he is keeping you at his mercy. If you return the call immediately or act too eager you are confirming that he is the man and validating his ego. If a guy takes the time to call you, take the time to return his call.

It's the thrill of the hunt.

It's not about what he can catch. It's about what he can hunt. In other words, instant gratification is not as satisfying as something that takes some work. If he is *only* about the hunt it will be obvious, and you can decide whether he's worth your time.

Realize the bottom line is validation.

You may wonder why men play games. A huge part of it is that they want validation. Men often get validation through the games they play. Women tend to make the mistake of trying harder when a guy is playing games. As a result, men get validation through games and continue to play them with other women.

Men often use mind games to gauge a woman's interest in them.

It's very childish, but we are all afraid of rejection. A man will resort to mind games just to see if a woman is interested in him. Often a man does this by pretending to be busy when a woman calls or texts him. This, in my opinion, is the worst way to determine if a woman is interested in a man. I have seen this backfire many times. I always recommend using the direct approach when trying to determine if a woman is interested in a man.

The guy can be emotionally unintelligent.

This has nothing to do with IQ. this is EQ (EMOTIONAL QUOTIENT). In fact, a low EQ is frequently associated with a HIGH IQ. So they can be SEEN as playing games, while the entire time they are just emotionally ignorant of how it is affecting the woman.

Remember that if he likes you, he won't play games.

Recognize that games are kept to a minimum when a guy truly likes a girl. This simple fact is crucial when it comes to weeding out the guys who are looking for a relationship from the guys who are looking for other things. If a guy is really into a girl, he won't want to play games, because he won't want to risk losing a good thing. If he's playing games, it's either about finding a hookup or validating his ego.

Chapter Thirteen

Happy being single is better than being miserable in a relationship.

If a relationship makes you miserable more than it makes you happy, it's time to close the door and find another door to open. Some people will deliberately make you miserable so you will close the door. Sometimes we keep a relationship going because of our children; but in most cases, it is better for the kids if they have two loving parents who are separated, rather than two parents who hate each other and are still married. Kids know when you're unhappy. In some instances separation is better for everyone. Then you can focus on making you and your children happy. Someone told me they would rather come from a broken family than be a part of one. If the relationship between parents isn't working, it will be reflected in behaviors and attitudes. Kids know when something is wrong. Miserable marriages harm kids and create traumas.

Some people can predict the future of a relationship, especially those who have had several relationships. Even though deep inside we want a relationship to continue, rationally sometimes we realize it's more beneficial for two parties to breakup rather than waste time and emotions.

Sometimes all we can do is leave in order to live.

Sometimes we feel like we don't have justification to end a relationship in the middle of it, even though we can see it will eventually fail. Sometimes leaving is the only option, especially when all else has been tried. Early break-ups can spare those involved pain and mental confusion and give them an opportunity to start another relationship with less accumulated emotional pain. Although the leaving part can be gut wrenching, in order to proceed with some normality in life it is necessary to do this after trying all possible ways to reconstruct a relationship. If you are married, and if you are sure love is gone, then there is no option but divorce. If there are children in the marriage, both parties need to be responsible enough to walk away with minimal negative effects on the children.

Being single gives you the opportunity to meet your one and only, and breaking up is *always* better than breaking down.

If your lover constantly threatens to leave you, tell him to go! He is not worthy of your love.

You may feel frightened when put in this position, but if he wants to leave, he is not right for you. Let him go and be strong. It will be less difficult than you imagine, and just think how you will feel when you meet a man who adores you and wants to stay with you forever. He is out there somewhere, waiting to meet you. Be brave and the guy that wants to leave go on his merry way.

If he says he wants to go and stays, then he's letting you know that he's a liar and willing to say outrageous things to keep you in your place. Or, he could be biding his time and hedging his bets. That way, whenever he decides it's the right time to take off he can say that he told you he was going to leave. This is someone who doesn't respect your relationship. Be aware that he is displaying the signs of being an abuser. Eventually, him telling you that he will leave, may not be enough to let him get his way, so be very aware of the things he says when he is angry. If he has to say mean things in order to "get your attention" then he has no idea how to properly communicate his feelings and express his anger. Is this the type of person that you want to be with for the rest of your life? Next time he threatens to leave, that should be your cue to get up and go. No one deserves to be with a person who keeps them in a relationship with threats. If you got married, would you want him saying that to your children? Would you want them to feel the uncertainty of not having a parent there? It doesn't matter if he acts upon these threats. The fact he can't find any better way to express his feelings should be a giant, barn sized red-flag. Tell him to either get some help or you will go find someone who values you and is willing to give you security. Emotional blackmail should never be tolerated or endured. Respect yourself.

Don't be a sex object.
Don't let her feel like that!

Men who disrespect you do not deserve a single second of your time. They have no respect for themselves, let alone for the women in their lives, and any respectful woman will stay well away from them. However, we can't expect a man to respect us, if we don't have respect for ourselves, and this shows in the way we carry ourselves, in the way we dress and in the way we talk. Even our body language is important. It is hard sometimes for a man to tell what a woman is saying with her smile. It's not the smile, but the way she smiles that he sees. It all comes down to body language. If a woman smiles and waves at a man, the wave can be the difference between saying hello, or it may be something else. When a woman goes out dressed like a "sex object" then she can't expect the same respect that a woman dressed up in more respectable attire would receive.

Women need Respect.

Respect is a principle that supports and sustains many aspects of marriage. If a husband respects and regards his wife with high esteem, it will make her feel good about her roles as woman and wife. Marriage will undoubtedly have its troubles, but if you remember the principle of "treat your wife as you would like to be treated," and visa versa, most problems can be resolved amicably before they get out of hand.

A woman needs her husband to show respect to her in the way he speaks to her and of her -- to always speak highly of her to others, and to never belittle her. Never speak sarcastically or sharply to her. Make sure she feels safe from any kind of abuse or harm, including verbal abuse from you or others. Treat her with at least as much deference and courtesy as you would an important business associate or celebrity. Be honest with her and respectful of her feelings. Give her the benefit of the doubt. Be patient and quick to forgive. Also, consider this advice: Confide in her. Share your deepest secrets and dreams with her, not others. Beware of situations that allow the formation of emotional attachments with other women.

Be sensually faithful to her.

Your wife cannot trust you completely or give herself completely to you unless she knows that she is your sole source of sexual gratification. Be absolutely faithful to her sensually, and let her know that you are. Absolute sensual fidelity to your wife means the following: Do not act as if you are still looking. Flirt only with your wife. Don't throw away what you worked so hard to have. Avoid all images of seductive women, including pornography as these images will drain the pleasure from your marriage. They will make you unsatisfied with her appearance and behavior. Eliminating them will allow your marital relationship to function as it was designed to, and will allow confidence, intimacy, beauty, and pleasure to fill your relationship. Sex is the glue of marriage. That glue should be binding you to her exclusively. Let her be your only one, and let her know that she is.

Involve her in important decisions:

In order to feel safe, a woman needs to feel some sense of control over the important decisions that affect her life. Think about how you would like to be involved in important decisions that affect the home and family. Make sure that she is a partner in all major decisions.

Chapter Fourteen

Some Women just pick the wrong guys!

I know this is painful, but it is the truth. Some women never learn from their failures. They just repeat the same mistakes. They become just attached to men who have attractive bodies, or other features. It doesn't matter how they look like inside. They just go after them. When they cheat on them or are abusing them physically and emotionally, they seem to like it. I've met a lot of women like that. They simply like those kinds of guys, and they *never* learn from their bad experiences.

Traditional psychoanalytic theory offered an intriguing, yet seemingly unlikely explanation for such self-destructive relationship choices. It said people who choose such partners derive pleasure from being mistreated. Simply stated, the choosers are masochistic. If the "pleasure principle" drives people, analysts argued, certainly this behavior follows the same rules. The therapist's task was to make the unconscious pleasure known to the patient--and then they would be free to choose a more appropriate partner.

But I never met anyone who received any pleasure at all, conscious or unconscious, from the abuse and neglect heaped on them by narcissistic or otherwise destructive partners. Rather, they were simply hurt over and over again.

This kind of woman must stop and think and tell herself, "If I choose to be with dishonorable males, pimps, players, thugs, and shot callers, I have absolutely no right to complain when they torch my emotions, abuse me, leave me pregnant and alone, jeopardize my safety and otherwise harm or hurt me. I have freedom of choice and I chose to be with them!" And then she must take her own words to heart and get out of the relationship.

Don't fake a Relationship!

Sometimes people fake a relationship; they do this for many reasons;

1. Because they afraid of being lonely, or
2. For financial support that they are receiving from a partner or
3. They are afraid of having the divorced title.
4. They cannot do anything except keep this relationship because they think it is the only chance for them to have a relationship, if you end the relationship.
5. They grow so attached to their partners that they forgot their lives before him or her.
6. They think they will never find anyone else who could possibly be interested in them or love them, or they don't leave. .
7. Because of sex, or
8. For their children!

They know what they go through, and they know every single deficit of their partner. With such a relationship they accept cheating, lying, and abuse and never complain. They just pretend that everything is perfect. They tell everyone around them they are okay, and they persuade themselves they are okay and that all relationships are like theirs. All men are cheating on their partners; all women are lying. Day by day, they become more depressed, have more low self esteem, more low self confidence, and more psychosomatic disorders (physical disease) that is thought to be caused, or made worse, by mental factors.

Remember: You can't change an unhappy relationship into a good one by taking abuse and hiding your emotions, but you *can* help a good relationship that's struggling become better if both partners want that and want help getting back on track.

Signs that you are in a fake relationship

Ignoring the truth

If you truly know that the relationship you are in is making you unhappy, but make no effort to exit from it, then you are in denial and are holding yourself hostage in a situation you do not have to endure.

Incorrect thinking

You think that all people are like you, that one of the rules of being in relationship is feeling miserable, or that your partner has the right to cheat on you, because everyone does that.

Making excuses

Making excuses for your partner's disappointing and bad behavior will keep you trapped and is another symptom of bad relationship addiction, especially if the excuses you produce do not back up the facts and are unrealistic.

No way out

If you do finally build up the courage to confront your partner and decide to leave him or her, but are overcome with fear, and therefore back off from the confrontation, you are a victim of addiction; because no matter what you attempt, you will always find yourself giving in and holding on to what you know is bad for you.

Psychosomatic Disorders

If you begin to suffer from both physical and mental discomfort once you decide to break up or when you think about being alone, after you break up, you need to seek help from a professional and get treatment.

What can I do to end a fake relationship?

1. Find a marriage counselor or other professional, and take that first step in accepting the fact that "YOU ARE IN A FAKE RELATIONSHIP" and that you need and want help to conquer it.
2. Start being a best friend to yourself and open the door to all the feelings you have kept locked up for so long. Keep in mind that there will always be a person who will be with you, who will never leave you, and who will always give you the strength, love and support you need, and that person is YOU.
3. REMEMBER: Life goes on even if you are hurt.
4. Never make 'someone' your God – she or he is only human like you.
5. Be concerned about your happiness and what makes you feel like a total person.
6. Remember the more time you take in making that decision to get out, the more time you will lose and never get back. It also means you may never know what you were capable of contributing to the world.
7. There are men who respect women and treat them like the ladies they are.
8. Encourage yourself frequently by setting a goal, and picturing yourself away from all the disappointment and closer to all the happiness and good health you need, desire and deserve as a person. Never give up and know that you are not alone, because you have yourself. Be your own best friend.

A real man never hits a woman, even with his tongue! The man who hits a woman lacks self- confidence.

Some males like to hit women. It gives them a sense of power and control. If you give yourself to one of these abusive males, most assuredly you will become a punching bag and a floor mat. It is critical that you learn how to detect and avoid these cretins!

Real men will never abuse you physically or emotionally. Unfortunately, we find some women accept this kind of relationship. I think they are more sick than their partners. Sometimes they say maybe he will change. I say, no. It is not like that. This kind of man NEVER changes, and there are a lot of signs showing exactly what kind of man he is.

Abuser tells Abused, "I love you."

Don't continue to sell yourself out to hear the occasional utterance of three hollow words that mean nothing to the abuser. You were not designed, built or destined for abuse, emotionally, physically or financially. If he is an abuser, there is no need to deliberate, because he IS NOT the one. Leave him now.

What are the signs that you're in an abusive relationship?

To determine whether your relationship is abusive answer the below questions. Place a check mark in the boxes that represent a "yes' answer. The more "yes" answers you have, the more likely it is that you're in an abusive relationship.

- ☐ You feel afraid of your partner much of the time?
- ☐ You avoid certain topics out of fear of angering your partner.
- ☐ You feel that you can't do anything right for your partner.
- ☐ You feel you always wrong. It is always your fault.
- ☐ You don't have the right to disagree.
- ☐ You've changed your core values, beliefs and goals to accommodate your partner in hopes that your relationship will no longer be problematic

Finders Keepers Losers Weepers

- ☐ If you discussed your partner he/she always mocks you.
- ☐ Your partner always threatens you he/she will disappear from your life if you didn't do what he is asking you.
- ☐ Your partner always fights if you didn't do what he wants even if you are sick.
- ☐ Your partner treats you so badly that you're embarrassed for your friends or family to see.
- ☐ Your partner ignores or put down your opinions or accomplishments.
- ☐ Your partner blames you for his own abusive behavior.
- ☐ Your Partner sees you as property or a sex object, rather than as a person.
- ☐ Your partner controls where you go or what you do! Even he/she asking for your email password to control your contacts and emails there.
- ☐ You've made drastic changes in your appearance hoping your partner will find you more attractive.
- ☐ You have a feeling of continuous frustration about the relationship (e.g., your emotional needs are not being met).
- ☐ You believe that you deserve to be hurt or mistreated.
- ☐ You wonder if you're the one who is crazy.
- ☐ You feel emotionally numb or helpless.
- ☐ You no longer have strong feelings about your partner but reminisce about the feelings you used to have.
- ☐ Your partner keeps you from seeing your friends or family.
- ☐ You've put extreme distance or totally cut off former close relationships you used to have with your other friends and/or family.

- ☐ Your partner limits your access to money, the phone, or the car especially after any auger as a punishment.
- ☐ Your partner constantly checks up on you. You find your partner everywhere you go without informing you.
- ☐ Your partner hurts you, or threatens to hurt or kill you.
- ☐ Your partner keeps on insulting you during every argument.
- ☐ Your Partner threatens to take your children away or harm them.
- ☐ Your partner threatens to commit suicide if you leave.
- ☐ Your partner forces you to have sex.
- ☐ Your partner destroys your belongings.
- ☐ Your partner disrupts you to not finish your work.

I think my friend is in an abusive relationship but I'm not sure.

Put a checkmark in the boxes that represent your friend's situation. The more check marks, the more likely it is that your friend is abused.

Does your friend:

- ☐ Receive frequent, harassing phone calls from their partner?
- ☐ Talk incessantly about their partner's temper, jealousy, or possessiveness?
- ☐ Have frequent injuries, with the excuse of "accidents?"
- ☐ Frequently miss work, school, or social occasions, without explanation?
- ☐ Dress in clothing designed to hide bruises or scars (e.g. wearing long sleeves in the summer or sunglasses indoors)?
- ☐ Seem afraid or anxious to please their partner?
- ☐ Go along with everything their partner says and does?

- ☐ Check in often with their partner to report where they are and what they're doing?
- ☐ Being restricted from seeing family and friends?
- ☐ Rarely go out in public without their partner?
- ☐ Have limited access to money, credit cards, or the car?
- ☐ Have very low self-esteem, even if they used to be confident?
- ☐ Show major personality changes (e.g. an outgoing person becomes withdrawn)?
- ☐ Seem depressed, anxious, or suicidal?

My friend is in an abusive relationship, how can I help?
- ☐ Ask if something is wrong.
- ☐ Express concern.
- ☐ Listen and validate.
- ☐ Offer help.
- ☐ Tell your friend it will be your little secret.
- ☐ Support his or her decisions.
- ☐ Don't wait for him or her to come to you.
- ☐ Stop judging or blaming.
- ☐ Don't pressure him or her.
- ☐ Don't give advice.

CHAPTER FIFTEEN

Forcing your wife to have sex with you is RAPE.

There is a myth that sexual violence is only carried out by strangers. In fact the majority of offences are committed by a man known to the woman. He may be a friend, a partner, a workmate, a relative, a neighbor or a person in authority.

Even if you are married, having sex without consent of the other person is rape. So if the husband forced his wife to have sex, I would consider that rape. Absolutely, it is rape, no doubt about it. If a woman says no, and the guy has sex with her anyway, it is rape by definition. Unfortunately, some igonarant men think they can force their wives to have sex with them. The wife may even feel she is wrong when she rejects her husband request, believeing she should fullfil his sexuel needs. Nevertheless, the husband can't compulse or force his wife into sexual marital rape. The husband may feel he has the right to insist that she should fullfil his right, and the husband has the right to be angry at her for this (in a proper way); *however, he still does not have the right to force her into sex, because this is marital rape.* It is well known that forcing someone to have sex brings physcial and emotional harm to a person. If a husband beats or scares his wife to force her to have sex, then he clearly abuses his wife's physical and emotional well being.

Any man whose wife continually or always refuses to have sex with him should not force her, by any means. But at the same time, that wife should not be shocked if he goes and finds it elsewhere. There are millions of women in the world, and they all possess the equipment required to satisfy his needs. If a woman doesn't want to ever have sex with her husband, then she probably also doesn't want to be married to him.

You are not always going to want to have sex. Agreeing that that he or she will be the only person you have sex with, does not mean that you have agreed to ALWAYS ALL THE TIME have sex with them no matter what.

Anyone who forces themselves on someone that obviously does not want sex is a rapist. It doesn't matter if you are her husband, if you hurt her by having sex with her without her consent, You are a rapist. Ask her if she wants sex. If she says no. so it means NO. Do not go against her will just to satisfy yourself.

It's rape even if the victim has an orgasm. Physiological response does not indicate consent.

Raping is one of the worst crimes of all. Something that can occur during rape is the victim can orgasm. I know this happens, but when the victim talks about the assault, it is rarely mentioned. I cannot imagine the confusion it must cause the victim.

"What is wrong with me? How could I possibly orgasm during such a horrible act?" the victim may ask.

It does happen, and there is a reason for it. It is not because the victim secretly wanted sex, and it is not because there is something wrong mentally with the victim. It simply happens because our bodies are designed to feel good when touched in a certain way. It is a normal reaction, and may or may not happen. Remember, you do not need intimacy to orgasm.

In one study about 5% to 21% of women interviewed reported having an orgasm when they were raped. Researchers have hypothesized the actual figure is probably a bit higher in reality, due to victims being understandably embarrassed both by the rape and by having achieved an orgasm during unwanted, forced sexual relations. It is estimated around 20% is a likely, *real world* figure.

Why would almost 1 in 5 women have an orgasm during a rape? It is just a fact that some of us will orgasm during a rape. The explanation is complex; but the bottom line is that whether or not a woman has an orgasm when she is raped, it is an experience that will haunt her unless she receives support, counseling and understanding in order to deal with the complex and deep emotions caused by the experience.

Rape is not always accompanied by other physical violence.

When a woman is sexually assaulted, she may react in various ways. Some women scream or fight back. Many become quiet and too shocked to speak or to cry out. Paralyzed by fear, they may be unable to resist. If violence is threatened, some may make the decision to struggle less in the hope of getting away with the least amount of physical harm. Consequently, they may or may not have torn clothes or signs of struggle afterwards. Verbal intimidation, threats or emotional blackmail may be used by the assailant. Therefore, a woman does not need to show physical injuries to prove she has been assaulted.

If this is something that has happened to you, you are not alone. You are not a freak, and you did not do anything wrong. If you are a victim of sexual assault, it was not your fault, you did not do anything wrong.

If you become a victim of sexual assault, remember it is *your* choice if you want to report it; and it is *your* choice if you want to seek counseling. I recommend both. Remember, rape is rape. The rapist is the only person who should be blamed.

Rape Is Not Woman's Fault.

Rape is not about sex -- it is about violence and control. No one is responsible for "making someone horny." A healthy, human response to wanting something from someone which they do not also want is not forcing them to give it to you, or making them feel that they are obligated to provide it.

Women who have suffered sexual attacks describe feeling:
- frightened
- guilty
- powerless
- angry
- ashamed
- depressed
- numb
- lacking self-confidence

Sometimes women have difficulty with eating or sleeping after they are raped. They may lack concentration and find this makes academic work difficult. Every woman reacts differently, and it is not unusual for feelings to change from day to day. In particular, there can be a long gap between the assault and the emotional reaction. It can be difficult to talk about the attack to friends or family, yet it is important to have understanding and support. It can be helpful to talk to a trained person in confidence – a counselor, psychologist, psychiatrist, or local Rape Crisis Centre.

Finders Keepers Losers Weepers

CHAPTER SIXTEEN

A woman who uses pregnancy to force a man to stay with her is manipulative, even if they are married!

Kids should NEVER be used as a bullying weapon. Having a child with someone doesn't increase your chances of having that person stick around. According to the United States census, in 2006, there were 12.9 million one-parent families — and 10.4 million of those were single mother families. In the U.S, eight out of ten teenage fathers do not marry their child's mother. I think you can see from those statistics alone, that if you have the idea that having a baby with a guy means you'll cement him to you, and your kid, it'd be wise to think twice. A whole lot of those single mothers thought the exact same thing.

The choice to be a parent is a huge one, about as huge as it gets in life, as any mother will tell you. Babies don't stay babies; and if you become a mother, you're a mother for the rest of your life. And when you choose to become a mother very young, you're choosing to parent at what will likely be the toughest time for you to do so, when you will have the least resources, the least cultural and community support (that's not your fault or the fault of teen moms, but that is how it is) and the least stability, which helps a whole lot when parenting. Stability helps you and it helps a kid who very much needs stability, not drama and chaos. When you choose to become a parent at a time when a relationship may be in crisis -- with the magical thinking a kid will fix things, something nearly everyone who has ever tried that has learned the hard way--this is false thinking -- you're choosing to do so at the worst time possible. Whether the father of your child sticks around or leaves, you and that kid -- who doesn't get a choice in any of this -- are tied to that person in some way for life.

I doubt that your health is impacted by having a sexual or romantic relationship with him or anyone else. I understand that when you're young and have very strong feelings about someone it can absolutely feel like without a romance with that person you can't survive, and the idea of losing that kind of relationship can make it feel like you can't even breathe. But you can. And you were breathing just fine just two months ago. Even if this guy doesn't stick around, after you get over a breakup, you'll be just fine again, and you have the ability to be healthy and happy without a relationship with him and even without romance at all. If you can't drop the desperation, you're unlikely to have a happy or a healthy life and relationship with him or with anyone else.

If becoming a mother is something that's part of what you want for your life, you could certainly start doing things that prepare you for that and help you plan for that, like being sure that you are in a stable relationship, doing the things in your life first that you want to do which will be harder or impossible to do with a child. Prepping for a good career that will support you and a child well is an important step.

If you don't love yourself,
how can you expect anyone else to love you?

Love yourself. Be yourself. Don't ever act like you are someone else just to have someone or to be in relationship. If your partner doesn't love as you are, there are many others who will love you because you are YOU. I'm not saying you shouldn't try to improve yourself. What I'm saying is you should know yourself, your deficits before your merits. In this way you will be able to improve yourself but still be yourself.

Don't ask your partner to do these things.

You've asked these questions, "Why doesn't he call me more often? Why doesn't he pursue me more diligently and why doesn't he show me that he loves me?"

Answer: "He's not into you! If you don't let him go and move on with your life, you will allow him to hinder and/or block your *true love* from finding you.

Love, caring, faith the relationship will survive—these are three things you cannot buy or ask for from your spouse.

You cannot ask your partner to love you. Love is not a choice or a decision.

You cannot ask your partner to take care of you, because even if you screamed to get it, he will not do it! Caring is something that comes from deep inside.

You cannot ask for faith in the relationship. A relationship is like a pair of scissors! One side cannot work without the other side!

CHAPTER SEVENTEEN

It's normal to feel a bit jealous and protective about your partner even if you have mutual trust.

Jealousy is a normal human emotion; however, it is one that can and will upset the balance of your life if you let it. Consider the reasons why it is occurring and (depending on the reasons) either try your best to overcome your jealousy, or move on from the situation. Jealousy is a very negative emotion that can and will destroy your peace of mind. It is best to get rid of it one way or another.

Normal jealousy has its basis in a real threat to a person's relationship with another. Most "normal" people experience intense jealousy when a valued relationship is threatened. On the other hand, jealousy is abnormal in two circumstances. First, jealousy is abnormal when it is not related to a real threat to a valued relationship, and rather to some inner trigger of the jealous individual. Such jealousy is also called delusional jealousy. Second, jealousy is abnormal when the jealous response is dramatically exaggerated or violent.

What causes jealousy?
If you think that you got jealous because of the way he talked to her or because of the way she smiled at him, then you are wrong. Jealousy, like most other emotions, is rooted internally, so a big part of

the problem lies within you, not as an extension of external conditions or circumstances. The following are possible root causes of jealousy:

- **Lack of self confidence**: The main cause behind feeling jealous is doubting your abilities or skills. If you're one hundred percent sure of yourself, you'll never suffer any jealous feelings and if you do, they will be minimal.
- **Poor self image**: Having a poor self image is another cause of jealousy. If you think believe you look bad or that you are not that handsome, then chances are you'll experience a feeling of jealousy whenever you meet someone better looking than you are.
- **Fear:** One of the root causes behind feeling jealous is being afraid. You may fear you will end up alone. You may have a fear of being shamed or a fear that you will lose the love your partner is providing you.
- **Insecurity**: Feelings of insecurity are the result of the two previously mentioned causes, a poor self image and a lack of self confidence. Feeling insecure about a relationship can be a strong reason for you to get jealous.

It's not right to read your partner's e-mails, text-messages or diary no matter how jealous you are.

Think. It is about trust. If you get jealous easily, you've probably had your trust broken. Most of the time the trust was broken in the past, and you inadvertently project your fear of being hurt again onto someone else. The question you need to ask yourself is whether this person (the person who you worry will hurt you) has ever done anything to break your trust in the past. If the answer is no, then it's important to give them credit for that, and not treat him or her like a criminal. If the person has broken your trust in the past, then it's time to forgive, or else jealousy will ruin the relationship.

Finders Keepers Losers Weepers

You can trust your partner and still be a bit jealous in some situations. My advice is to never rely on intuition when you are jealous, or you'll become an illusionist, trust your partner and don't let jealousy get the best of you, and remember that if someone is going to hurt you, there's nothing you can do to stop it anyway. No amount of nagging, monitoring, accusation, snooping, or guarding will prevent you from being hurt. If you believe in someone, believe in them completely and give them all your trust. Giving the benefit of the doubt is essential for any relationship to work. And if you really don't trust them, if you really feel that the person is weak, deceptive, or otherwise untrustworthy, then don't associate with that person. You deserve better.

You have a right to react jealously if your partner gives you reason for that.

Those were the days, when your husband had eyes only for you. It made you feel very special and truly loved. But now you find that he makes no bones about the fact that he's checking out other women. And if there's one thing a woman finds most annoying, it is that her man feels compelled to survey the scenery in the room, and we're obviously not talking about décor.

Case One Says:

"My boyfriend goes on a trip to India with a woman who he says it is only a business relationship, but she thinks they are a couple. They sleep in the same hotel room. He can't contact me when she is around during the trip. He spends Saturday night and Valentine's Day weekend with this woman, but according to him he made it clear to her that they are only friends. He often spends the night at her house, but sleeps in another room. She does his laundry, dispenses his meds and keeps his dog. My boyfriend says I should not be jealous or have an issue with this situation."

Finders Keepers Losers Weepers

Case Two Says:

"I find it frustrating when I'm talking to my partner about something serious or telling him something that begs a response and I look up and find him staring dumbstruck or totally absorbed – not in what I'm saying – but in the leggy redhead walking past or the curvaceous blonde sashaying down the supermarket aisle."

Many women like these women are unsure whether to take these matters up with their spouses or boyfriends, or to just ignore it. Some take it very seriously – as if looking is tantamount to cheating or straying. But it doesn't have to be so.

Women may not make it so obvious when they admire a man. This could be for either of two reasons. First, no matter how good looking or attractive, a man may be, he rarely evokes the kind of reactions and response that a beautiful or sexy woman evokes in a man. Second, women are subtle I both their reactions to the opposite sex and in hiding their true feelings.

If your husband is looking at other women, analyze it as objectively as you can. See if you can fathom why he does it, and why it gets to you. As long as he doesn't have any hidden agenda and his intentions are aboveboard, go the 'ignorance is bliss' way. You may be getting hot under the collar about his wandering eyes because deep down, you're insecure about him and his intentions? If this is so, talk to him about it, and tell him how you really feel.

Chapter Eighteen
Nothing is forever.

If you are just starting a new relationship, keep doing the things that are making you successful. If you and she both respect the fact that feelings, including love, *can* and *do* change based on how one is treated, you will never become complacent.

Remember, a perfect relationship is not a relationship where everything goes smoothly, but a relationship that grows constantly. There are times in any relationship where you can't stand your partner. This does not mean it is a bad relationship.

Every relationship has its little ups and downs. It is normal, even in our sexual life. Researchers say there are four stages we get through during our relationship:

- Love for love: We find this stage always in the beginning of the relationship.
- Love for sex: Men usually reach this stage before women. This stage means that you feel love when you have sex with your partner.
- Sex for love: That means you have sex in order to feel love.
- Sex for sex: In this stage you have sex as a duty or you just have sex for sex.

These stages show that in the third and the last stages, your relationship is really facing a problem. You must try to fix it with your spouse. But remember every relationship goes up and down and with good communication you will overcome any problem.

Leaving for Living

Not all relationships are meant to be. Divorce can be the best solution for our life problems. Divorce not always means a broken heart. In some cases, divorce is the ONLY solution to get your life back. But in a lot of cases divorce is like a signed suicide contract, especially if you are still in love with your partner. There are different reasons for a relationship to end. It can be due to the jealous nature of a spouse, misunderstanding, cheating, or over possessiveness. In this day and age of drive-in marriages, quick divorces are no longer shocking. Many marriages end up in divorce.

Fate controls who walks into your life, but you decide who walks out, who stays and who you refuse to let go.

You need some real work to keep your man in love with you, because a lasting relationship is not something that will just naturally happen. You need to work at it. If you are in a relationship and want to avoid breaking up, you should know how to make him stay in love with you.

Be a homemaker.

In today's modern world most women are career women, and this is not a bad thing as long as women do not neglect their responsibilities at home. Men can offer a helping hand at home; but of course, women should be the main homemaker. To make him stay in love with you, be a good homemaker. Take care of the home and cook meals for the family. And for men be a good helper; find a task and make it your permanent homemaker skill.

Be a friend.

Aside from your love and affection, your partner needs your companionship. Your partner needs someone to talk to and someone to share the good and bad happenings in his or her life. You are there to laugh with your partner, to celebrate your partner's accomplishments, and to uplift your partner in times of defeat or failure. Be a friend and you can make your parnet stay in love with you.

Doll up for your man.

Physical looks matter to most men. You do not have to be a supermodel beauty, but being presentable and taking good care of your looks can be very helpful if you want to make him stay in love with you. Women who are not concerned with their looks and figure will eventually lose the interest of their men. A woman who knows how to carry herself is always an attractive woman. This applies to men too. If you ask your woman to be an attractive woman, you must also be an attractive man.

Be supportive:

Men are not always tough, and there are times they need the support of their woman to boost their confidence or to keep them going. It is important that you are supportive of your man in whatever endeavor he wants to take. Make him stay in love with you by being supportive.

If a woman has any problems at home or at work, the man should also try to be a supportive. He should listen to her and to her problems and not try to give her solutions. (You can do that later.) Just listen to her and let her feel you are there for her.

Give him his alone time.

Men need their private space to grow as a person. Although couples should be together most of the time, your man needs his alone time once in a while. Give him time to unwind and discover new things. Men sometimes need time to open up, and you should respect that and give him time to sort through his thoughts.

CHAPTER NINETEEN

My partner wants to break up, but I don't !

Love is a relationship where give and take rarely occurs in equal degrees. You may find someday that somewhere along the way your relationship has changed, and your partner is no longer the ardent lover he used to be. If you feel that he's the one for you, here are some steps you can take to give your relationship a fighting chance.

Give him space.

Give him a break if he simply needs to have some time by himself. Men tend to be very protective of their private space. After a while in a relationship your partner may feel that he is losing himself or getting overwhelmed with all things related to you "especially in the beginning of relationship". So if he expresses a desire to take a vacation by himself or take a job in a new city, give in calmly. He will not only appreciate the time-out, but who knows? The days spent away from you may make him realize that he still wants to be with you.

Don't go chasing after him, but stay in touch.

If he has indeed gone for a break, don't keep calling or mailing him a hundred times a day. Act cool. Don't be in a rush to return his calls; however, if there are three messages from him waiting on your answering machine, call back to say a casual 'hi'. This will leave him a way to return back to you without you appearing too desperate to get back together.

Discover yourself while he is away.

I know it is difficult when you feel your life is not like it used to be, but there are a lot of things you can do to enjoy your life while your partner is gone. Learn new skills or pick up a hobby. Get involved in projects you have been meaning to do in the past. but had not found time to do. These interests will not only enrich your life, they will help your partner realize you have a life without him; and believe me, nothing turns on a man as much as a confident, mature woman appreciated by the people around her. So try to find *yourself* while he is away. A lot of women unfortunately think they are incomplete without their partners, but that's not true; so take this chance to discover your competence, as well as your completeness. while he is away.

Bond with close friends

Surround yourself with friends and people who care for you. Understand the pattern. Arrange to meet a friend every other day. This is the time you can really call upon your closest friends, and tell them to be your anchor and support. Avoid unsupportive people who want to say "I told you so." You do not have to put up with people who say "I always knew he was no good," or "I knew she was cheating on you." Politely tell them, that even if your relationship ended, you are an adult and you will take full responsibility for your actions and decisions. Arguing about these things at this point, does *not* help the cause *anyway;* and it only makes you feel silly, which is unnecessary.

Finally: the most important thing to know is "There is no single guaranteed way to win back the love of your partner, no matter what any of the relationship books tell you. What may bring another estranged couple together may not work for you simply because people, circumstances and the dynamics of relationships are different. So when you find your partner moving away, and you feel you still love him, take a deep breath and believe in yourself, believe in who you are, and remember he loved you because of what you already have. He loved you because you are YOU. Don't try to change who you are, just enhance yourself; and eventually, you may find that your love has come back to where he truly belongs – with you. If he doesn't return, it's his loss. You will find someone else.

My partner left me.
I feel like it's the end of the world!

Maybe you feel it is the end of the world, but it is not! Life does not end and this means a new beginning, not an ending. We have the intrinsic ability to mend our hearts and get on with our lives.

After breaking up all we think is" What am I going to do all alone?" Everything around is reminding you of him. One woman told me after *her* break-up she was working *more* than eighteen hours a day just to avoid returning home where she had think about her life before the break-up. She lost both sleep and appetite prior to finding a way out of her grief.

Time
All wounds heal. Time is what makes the difference. Some heal fast. Others take some time. Eventually everyone heals. And you *can* do *your* part to make the transition to being 'happily single' *again..* Just try to cope. Don't let a break-up *break* you.

Maybe time is a great healer, but you must play your role.

Talk

Finders Keepers Losers Weepers

For some people talking about their ex(s) hurts more than breaking up, but you cannot underestimate what talking can do. Try to open your heart to supportive people in your life, such as your mom and your close friends, or seek professional help. These sources will able to help you and perhaps show you what you weren't able to see because you were in love. One woman told me that after she spoke with her close friends she wondered what she was doing in the relationship. She discovered the guy she thought was the one, was making moves on her friends on the side. They couldn't tell her before the break-up, because they didn't want to hurt her feelings.

List your happy times. Then list your bad memories.

Why the list of happy moments *before* bad memories? Because we make a big mistake right after a break-up. We only think about the bad things. Then in piecemeal fashion, we find ourselves thinking about the good times, and this means healing takes a long time.

Next, think how lucky you are to be out of a bad relationship. Think about how much fun you had when you were single, and look at other people in bad relationships. Then be thankful you are not like them *anymore.*

Make list of his or her weaknesses and your strengths.

Make a list of everything you stopped doing because you were in love. People say love is blind, but this just isn't true. Love *has sharp* vision, *but* we are wearing *dark glasses* to avoid seeing our partner's deficits. When love is over, take off that dark glasses and see the truth. The truth is *you* deserve someone better.

Revenge

Paul told me he wasn't able to stop thinking about his ex! He decided needed revenge. He put her photo in front of him as a toss game background. *Then* he *replaced* her photo with her weakness list. After that, he thought about the good things he had done for her. He was able to recognize his strengths. He removed the toss game and forgot her. He found the best revenge was living well.

As vague as that is, it's pretty clear that if you are happy with your current situation in life, it means that your life is a lot better without your ex. Be happy with your life and life's choices. Make your peace with your current situation and be content. True happiness shows on your face, through your smile and through your laughter.

Forgive

When you stop blaming forgiving, you restart your heart and get over the break-up. Forgiveness helps you to feel better about yourself as a human being, gives you the chance to learn from the mistakes you may have made in the relationship.

Support

Some people cannot share their problems face-to-face. But they *can* seek help online. There are chat rooms and message boards online where people recovering from break-ups get support.

You can also share your passion and thoughts in web sites made for that. When you write your thoughts and find people share them with you, it may make you feel better.

Pray

This one's *not* for atheists! Visit mosque "masjed," church, or temple. Such places provide you with the peace and quiet you need.

Don't jump right into another relationship. Give yourself the chance to find another one.

Don't be in a rush to find a substitute for your ex-boyfriend. While it is alright to meet new people and have a different social circle while emerging from a break-up, don't charge headlong into a new relationship. These rebound affairs never work; and in most cases, they leave you feeling worse than ever.

Don't regret it's finished. Be glad it happened. Remember, being single gives you the chance to find your one true love.

You are *not* the first one with a broken heart, and you won't be the last. Force yourself to be positive. Remember that happy and single is better than miserable and in relation. A break-up is *not* the end of the world. It might be the beginning. Being single again gives you the chance to find your one true love.

I'm obsessed with my Ex! What can I do to let go?

You tell me, "I can't stop thinking about my ex. I replay the scenes of my break up again and again in my mind just to figure out how it happened!"

If you feel like this, you are getting obsessed with your ex. It is time to let go!

Don't blame yourself.

> *"If only I could lose some more weight."*
> *"If only I didn't say what I said last time."*

You could go on and waste your time and your life. Just accept it. You have split. He left. It's not your doing. It is not your fault.

Accept the reality.

Accept what has happened. I know it is hard, but it is *not* impossible. You still have the right to feel sad, angry, and completely miserable, if you like. But after a self-stipulated time, open the drapes and let the sun in, and open the windows and breathe in fresh air. Restart your life. Restart your heart.

Get rid of everything that reminds you of your ex.

A good way to let go of the past is to sweep away all its reminders. This means not only emptying your bathroom cabinet of his aftershaves and toothbrushes and her day cream, but also getting rid of things like joint credit cards and joint bank accounts. Remove him or her from your speed-dial, and de-list from 'favorites' lists.

Let your fears go.

Forget your apprehension and worry about being alone and how you'll cope. You must learn to trust again. Trust yourself and your instincts. One, two three or even more broken relationships doesn't mean that you should close yourself off from loving again. Relationships may involve agony, but they also involve ecstasy. Life wouldn't be complete without a healthy dose of both.

Find YOU as a new friend.

This is the best time to come back to the person who matters most – you! Take time off from every other concern and focus on the person you are. Focus on your priorities, the goals you want to set for yourself and the person that you eventually want to become. Often a relationship makes us overly involved in another person and we lose focus of ourselves. This is the right time to start working towards regaining your own identity. Better still, see if you can translate your aspirations into something concrete – like learning a new skill, taking up a hobby you always found interesting, or even relocate to a new city and a new job.

Sorry my ex. You cannot be my friend.

When your partner "who is your ex now" offers to remain friends, this may his way of dealing with his guilt. Keep away from this trick. This will not only keep you tied to dead relationship, it will also delay the healing process.

Chapter Twenty

*Love in one direction is a kind of suicide.
Love in one direction cannot be love.*

"He doesn't love me as much as I love him."

If you've ever said this phrase, you were living or are living in an unbalanced relationship. It's tough when you fall hopelessly in love with a person whose feelings clearly aren't as deep as yours.

You may tell a woman that you love her, but a woman has an instinct that tells her whether you are as crazy about her as you are about him. (A man may also feel this way.)

When you suspect that his or her devotion doesn't run as deep as yours, you need to take control of the situation and change that. You possess all the tools you need to make him or her fall hopelessly in love with you. All you need to make it happen is the required insight.

Everyone wants to love and to be loved. It is painful when you are in love with someone who doesn't love you back. My advice for you is, don't live with someone like this you are *nothing* to them if they are *everything* to you.

Once you stop seeing the world with your ex's eyes, you will see the real world.

Have you recently ended a relationship or are you recently divorced? Are you thinking about dating again? Putting yourself back into the dating scene is a good idea. But how do you know when it is time to start a new relationship?

1. Don't start a new relationship if you still fantasize about getting back with your partner. You are not truly available for another relationship. Is there really a possibility of reconciliation? Or are you making up the possibility? If there really is a possibility, then it is certainly *not* time to even date. If the relationship is really over, then you need to fully accept this *before* moving on to *another* relationship. As long as you are in denial about the relationship being over, you are *not* fully available for another relationship.

2. Get rid of everything that reminds you of your Ex. Before you start a new relationship, you must let your ex go. You don't need that extra clutter in your life. Junk all the souvenirs, cards and memorabilia. You really don't want to go down that road. In fact, if she wrote you a letter to break up, that's the first thing to hit the flames. However, if he was a lavish lover, and you really dig the cool bracelet he gave you, don't let your heart rule your head. Keep it! There will come a time when you can flaunt it without thinking of him with that ache in your heart. *That* will be the time you're *truly* over him.

3. Create a happy environment. Surround yourself with positive people. Watch your favorite cartoon (even Tom and Jerry can do wonders) or a perky sitcom. Play funky music that can pep

you up a bit. Avoid convoluted soaps and slow songs that make you long for your partner. Break-up survival tip? Serials you used to watch *together* and playing *"our song"* are best avoided.

4. Start your own life. Your love life isn't the most happening thing at the moment. So what? You can't have it all. Look at all the areas of your life that are sailing along smoothly. Revel in them. Seize happiness from little things like a good bargain or a great boss and, of course, your wonderful family and friends! In fact, now that you don't have to invest time and energy in your love life, use *this* opportunity to strengthen and cement your relationships with friends and family.

My husband left me for another woman.

When your husband leaves you for another woman, you may feel as if you will never get your life back. But have faith in the fact that you are not alone. Every day millions of women around the world are coping with the same kind of abandonment, and they are picking up the pieces of their life – so will you!

Face the reality.

Accept the fact no matter how impossible it may seem. Allow yourself to get upset. Take time to cry if you feel like it, and get as miserable as possible. The grieving process is important if you are to move on to the next stage of healing.

Stop blaming yourself.

It did not happen because you were too fat, too thin, too busy or too lazy. It did not happen because the other woman was too sexy or too intelligent. Understand that what happened has happened. Do not blame yourself. Your biggest priority is to pull yourself together and look after your kids, if you have any.

Pamper yourself.

Have breakfast in bed. Pamper that body of yours. Take a bubble bath, paint your toes, pluck your eyebrows, buy yourself something pretty! You can find a bouquet of flowers at the grocery store for under $10. Watch your favorite movie, order food from outside. Relax while reading a book, and eat some chocolates.

Look after yourself.

Eat a healthy diet. Continue to exercise if you were in the habit of doing so before your husband left. Above all, stay away from unhealthy choices like rebound sex, alcohol or drug abuse. None of these things will make your pain go away. They will merely take away your natural ability to heal yourself. Pick up a new hobby or learn a new language. Join a course in which you were always interested, but for which you never had time. If you don't have a job, look for one.

Stop thinking about the other woman.

An essential part of getting on with life after your husband leaves you for another woman is to let go of the thoughts of the other woman. If you don't know her, you may be tempted to fantasize about her attractiveness and sex appeal. If you know her, you might be assailed with emotions of jealousy and betrayal. If you find you cannot put these thoughts behind you on your own, seek the help of a counselor. It is much easier for professional therapists to come up with effective solutions that will help you to cope with your feelings of abandonment and betrayal.

Don't succumb to a rebound relationship.

Rebound affairs never work, because you are just *not* emotionally ready for a *new* relationship. *And* even if you *aren't* serious about it yourself, it is *grossly unfair* to the other person, who may *not* be aware of your *real* feelings.

Take a vacation.

A change of scene and people can speed up the healing process when you are trying to cope with the end of a relationship. Go for the vacation you always intended to take, but could not fit into your schedule, *because* of your ex-partner. Explore new surroundings, culture and cuisine; and you will *realize* that this world is *too vast* and life *too short* to waste time grieving over the past.

Remember, the other woman didn't steal him. He is not a purse. What happened was *his* choice. He chooses who he dates, who he is sexual with, who he has relationships with and with whom he does not have relationships.

Chapter Twenty-One

Living in hell is better than living with a selfish person.

Living with selfish person is Hell itself. In love don't give without *taking*, and don't take *without* giving. Love is meant to be a mutual relationship. If you only give, you are spoiling your partner. If you only take, you are selfish and using your partner.

Don't be like the woman who told me, "The guy who loves me is a selfish slag. It's hard to walk away because he was sweet as pie in the beginning. Then he stole everything from me, belittled me and everything had to be about him. He was jealous, insecure, and basically I only think he *loved* the sex. It's a tough situation. I still can't get this guy to leave me alone. He'll beg and plead even cry to manipulate me until I give in and start thinking he cares, then he goes right back to bailing on me when we're supposed to hang out, and toys with my head."

If it is always him and his career, his car, his house (or her's) and it is *never* about *you*, something is wrong. Does your partner ever even ask how *your* day went or how *you* are feeling? No. You have to spend all your time catering to your partner. Unequal relationships are no good. Selfish people are *incapable* of feeling the type of emotion

Finders Keepers Losers Weepers

that produces the actions that make *others* feel loved. The single *most important person* in *their* world is *them*. It does happen, not always successfully, that they are fortunate enough to meet that certain person that knocks them off their high horse straight into love. However, genery, a selfish person cannot love someone else. Love is an action word. It *requires* selflessness.

A selfish person can't love. Most selfish men and women have been raised that way. When they get into a relationship, instead of wanting a husband or a wife, they want a mother or a father. Always remember, you *can't* change a person. They can *modify* their behavior to meet your needs out of love and respect, but *inherent* personality traits will *not* change. Move on, because he or she will always have himself or herself. They can't love *you*. They *won't* love you. Focus on yourself, and get out there and find the one who *can* love you.

Chapter Twenty-Two

It's hard to live with someone who has emotional obsessive-compulsive disorder.

Maybe this is the first time you have ever heard the term *emotional obsessive-compulsive disorder*. This is probably because there *is* no disorder called *emotional obsessive-compulsive disorder*. But it exists in life. What is EOCD? It is a potentially disabling illness that traps people in endless cycles of repetitive thoughts and behaviors. People with OCD are plagued by recurring and distressing thoughts, fears, or images (obsessions) that they cannot control. People with EOCD can't trust *anyone*. They always think their partner is cheating on them. The basis of most good relationships is *trust*.

If you can't trust the other person, the relationship is *never* going to run very deep. Building trust takes time, *especially* when one or both parties have been hurt in the past.

A relationship is a decision between two people, and without *trust* no relationship can start. How can you *love* someone you can't trust? It also takes a pretty resilient personality to constantly reassure and accommodate an insecure, mistrusting mate. Of course, there *is* such a thing as being *too trusting;* and there *are* those that know how to take advantage of that.

Why do some people have EOCD?

Fear is one of the sets of basic or instinctive emotions like joy, anger and sadness. All of those emotions play a major part in personal relationships. If someone grew up in family where the parents were divorced because of trust issues, that person may automatically fear trusting *other* people. If the mother cheated on the father, the son may grow up having trust problems toward all women and vice versa.

A Person may also develop a fear of trusting people if they saw one of their friends suffering badly because of trust issues. It doesn't really matter if he was the one betrayed or if he saw someone else suffering from a betrayal. In both cases, the subconscious mind will *still* consider trusting other people *dangerous.*

Some parents feed their children with false ideas about trust. These parents describe what has happened *to them,* thinking *this* is what will happen to *everyone else;* and then the child grows up having trust issues.

If a girl thinks she should never trust a guy, her subconscious mind will let her fall in love with a liar who will then cheat on her, just to proof to her that she should not trust anyone. That's why some women tend to always get into abusive relationships. They think *all men* are abusers. Their subconscious minds always find abusive men to *support* their beliefs. I am not saying people are angels. There *are* people you should not trust. However, there are also *good people* out there. You can't trust *everyone*, but you *can trust* the right one.

Reasons given for not trusting

1. I have been hurt too much in the past, and I refuse to be hurt again now or in the future.
2. People are out to get all they can from you, so avoid them to survive.

3. As soon as you let your guard down, you will be stepped on again.
4. No one is to be trusted.
5. You always get hurt by the ones you love.

We always hear above from EOCD people; People need to develop the following behavior traits, attitudes and beliefs in order to develop trust:

The first step is to **write down the reasons you do not trust the person:** Weight the importance of the items on the list with a scale from one to three based on how severe they are. If you have even one item that is in the most severe category, you may not be able to regain the trust. Look over your list, and if it is composed of only a few minor to medium offenses, then you should be able to work on regaining your trust of the person. But, if the list is long with several items that are rated as very severe, you will need to evaluate whether you want to attempt to regain trust of the person.

Self-disclosure of negative self-scripts: Your disclosing of your inability to feel good about yourself and your perceived lack of healthy self-esteem are essential in reducing miscommunication or misunderstanding between you and the significant others in your life. This self-disclosure reveals to the others your perspective on obstacles you believe you bring to relationships. This sheds the mask of self-defensiveness and allows the other to know you as you know yourself. It is easier to trust that which is real than that which is unreal or hidden.

Becoming vulnerable: This enables you to be hurt by others who know your weaknesses and strengths. This is an essential step in trust-building between people. It lays the cards on the table in a gamble that in such total self-revelation the others will accept you for who you really are rather than for whom they want you to be. In order to get to full self-disclosure you must take the risk of being vulnerable to others. This is an important building block in trust development.

Letting go of fear: Fear restricts your actions with others. Letting go frees you of behavioral constraints that can immobilize your emotional development. Fear of rejection, fear of failure, fear of caring, fear of success, fear of being hurt, fear of the unknown and fear of intimacy are blocks to the development of trust relationships and can impede relationship growth if not given appropriate attention and remedial action. You should understand that even when you begin to trust this person and decide to continue your friendship or relationship again it will never be *exactly* like it was. It *could* improve. Moving on from the betrayal *might* make your bond stronger, but it could *also* become *worse*.

Self-acceptance: Accepting who you are and what your potential is, is an important step in letting down your guard enough to develop a trusting relationship with others. If you are so insecure in your identity that you are unable to accept yourself first, how can you achieve the self-revelation necessary to develop trust? Self-acceptance through an active program of self-affirmation and self-love is a key to the development of trust.

CHAPTER TWENTY-THREE
About marriage and divorce

Marriage is *never* a solution to problems in a relationship; In fact, marriage can be the source of the problems. A couple should *only* get married when they love each other, trust each other, and can be honest to each other. Most importantly, must understand one another and accept their partner as he or she is.

One woman described her experience like this.

"As I was walking down the aisle, I realized we shouldn't be getting married. I knew I wasn't ready, and I kept praying to God that when the pastor asked if there was anyone who had an objection, someone would stand up and say so. But no one did. So I went through with it, hoping things would get better. But they didn't. They became worse! Finally, we divorced."

You probably know people like this woman. Before getting married you must *be sure* about your feeling and know if you can *really* handle this commitment *or not*. Before you decide to get married, be sure that you are *absolutely dedicated* to your partner. If you are unsure, don't push too quickly into marriage. You don't want to get married if you're *only* half-sure. Too many people get married for the wrong reasons or are not emotionally prepared for it. They walk into marriage thinking it is the solution to all of their problems. While it may be a solution to *some* problems, it can create a host of *other problems* that are unique and challenging to married life.

How do you save your marriage when divorce seems imminent?

Face it.

The first step towards stopping an imminent divorce is to acknowledge there is a conflict and there are issues that need to be sorted out as early as possible. Very often, partners believe that as long as the conflict is not out in the open, the marriage can limp along somehow. Take your courage in both hands and broach the matter with your spouse.

Discover what's wrong.

Make a list of what is troubling your marriage, and ask yourself how you got to this point. Take your thoughts to your partner, and then let your partner express their thoughts. This kind of communication can help you and your partner find the primary source of the present conflict so you will be able to solve it. But be careful while discussing the source of conflict in your marriage. Be careful to maintain an objective stance. Avoid getting caught up in the endless cycle of accusations and counter-accusations. A good way to do this, is to refrain from statements starting with "you." For instance do not say, "You do not appreciate my work" or "You spend too much time working." Instead, try to say, "I would feel much more valued in my marriage, if my work is appreciated," or "It would mean so much to me if we could spend more time with each other." Charging the other person with bringing about the cause more of a crisis in your marriage. It will not lead the discussion anywhere that is helpful to eiter of you.

Find solutions.

Discuss what each of you can do to improve the relationship, which will, in turn, entail bringing some amount of change within oneself. Each of you will have to give a little in terms of time and effort. Each of you will need to make some changes in his or her priorities and principles if the marriage is to be saved. Here, more than anywhere, mutual co-operation is a *must*, especially since the stakes are so high.

Seek 'people help' if required.

Involve people you both trust. Family help, professional help and close-friend help can work wonders for troubled marriages. It is imperative that both spouses are willing to fix the marriage, since any workable solution will need the co-operation of both partners. If you both feel your marriage is worth saving, give it your best shot. Begin with a positive attitude and spare no effort in working things out.

What are the signs your marriage is in trouble?

You hear your own silence.

Living in silence is often the first warning sign that all is not right in the relationship. You no longer seem to have anything to say to your spouse. It seems like you are two people who have nothing to share anymore.

You no longer do anything fun or interesting together.

Consider this a warning sign on the health of your marriage. It is natural that over time, you will each find your own niche in the relationship. It is *unusual* for the spouses to give up *all* shared interests.

You are the last person to know.

A disintegrating marriage is strongly characterized by an increasingly widening communication gap between partners. In these situations your partner will stop sharing information about his or her social and professional life with you. You will find out about your spouse's achievements at work, or problems with family members, from second or third-hand sources, such as your partner's co-worker or neighbors of your partner's parental home.

There is a lack of trust.

You no longer trust each other. Mutual trust is the cornerstone of any meaningful relationship, including marriage. If you find yourself constantly doubting your partner's whereabouts, or if your spouse suspects you of infidelity, something is deeply wrong in your marriage.

You feel no need to look 'perfect' for your partner.

If you find your spouse has undergone a sudden sharp decline in appearance and hygiene, it could be because your partner no longer cares whether you find them desirable. This complete lack of interest is an indication your spouse is no longer happy in the marriage and sooner or later is likely to opt out.

You keep arguing about the same issues in the same way.

If discussions about your relationship seem to be stuck in a rut with the same arguments again and again, it is evident your marriage is in trouble. The inability to communicate thoughts and feelings effectively is often the initial step toward a breakdown in a relationship. Enlist the help of a marriage counselor if you both seem unable to resolve issues on your own.

Do you need a marriage counselor?

Marriage counseling, also called couples therapy, is a type of psychotherapy. Marriage counseling helps couples — married or not — recognizes and resolves conflicts and improves their relationships. Through marriage counseling, you can make thoughtful decisions about rebuilding your relationship or, in some cases, regarding going your separate ways. Marriage counseling is usually provided by clinical social workers or licensed therapists known as marriage and family therapists. These therapists have graduate or postgraduate degrees — and many choose to become credentialed by the American Association for Marriage and Family Therapy (AAMFT).

Marriage counseling is often short term. Marriage counseling typically includes both partners, but sometimes one partner chooses to work with a therapist alone. The specific treatment plan depends on the situation.

What Type of Couple Gets the Most From Marriage Counseling?

- ☐ Young couples.
- ☐ Non-sexist couples.
- ☐ Couples who are still in love.
- ☐ Couples who are open to therapy and change.

What type of couple receives the least from marriage counseling?

- ☐ Couples who wait too long before seeking help.
- ☐ Marriages with one or the other spouse set on getting a divorce.
- ☐ Married individuals who are closed to any suggestions that may save the marriage.

What are the signs that your marriage is in trouble and that you might need counseling?

Finders Keepers Losers Weepers

1. **Communication is a problem:** So much has been written about how important communication is in any relationship. In a marriage, it assumes even more significance. If you and your partner are unable to satisfy this most fundamental of prerequisites, then you need a marriage counselor to guide you as to how to communicate effectively. He will provide you with suggestions for open and effective communication. How you can provide an environment conducive to sharing with and listening to your spouse.
2. **You are contemplating divorce:** If you and your spouse have had problems on several fronts and are talking divorce, look before you leap. If you haven't yet seen a marriage counselor it might still not be too late. Getting out of a relationship is not a solution unless it is under extenuating circumstances. If you have some serious issues, you might face the same problems in another relationship. So it's best you seek help now and resolve them. Give it a chance with someone who is trained to help couples like you and you may be surprised at the results.
3. **Mental disorder:** If you or your spouse has a mental illness or depression of some sort, you should seek professional help immediately. Apart from a physician or mental health expert who would administer medical advice and treatment, you will also need counseling on how to cope with the situation. It is very difficult to deal with a spouse suffering from depression and you will require all the help you can get.
4. **Infidelity issues:** If you have discovered your spouse is cheating on you or if you have been the unfaithful one, it might help to talk about it to a marriage counselor. After all, it is a situation fraught with tension and anxiety, and you may feel the need of having an impartial and unbiased third party to talk you through the problem. First, you must decide, that you are going to give the relationship a chance.
5. **Conflict resolution:** If you find it extremely difficult to work through conflicts or there are certain issues that don't seem to

get sorted out, it might pay to solve them with the expertise only a marriage counselor can provide. He will provide you with useful tools and strategies to deploy when faced with conflict.

6. **Your spouse sees reality, but doesn't care:** You can communicate until you're blue in the face, but if your partner doesn't care how you feel or whether the relationship is healthy, then your marriage may be over. Communication is secondary to caring.
7. **You have different visions of your future:** He wants a four million dollar home on oceanfront property. You want to live in a cottage in the country. He wants six children. You'd rather be childfree. He wants his mom and aunt to live with you in his four million dollar home. You can barely tolerate Christmas dinner together.
8. **Dissatisfied:** If one or both of you are seriously unhappy with the state of your marriage, counseling may help. There may be various factors, some suppressed, as to why you feel this way about your marriage. A marriage counselor will help you to probe beneath the surface and to get in touch with your deeper emotions, thus finding a way to help you and your spouse.
9. **Incompatibility:** If you have been faced with serious issues, sexually or otherwise, that make you think you are totally unsuited for each other, seek help before contemplating something drastic. If the two of you made the decision to get married, things couldn't always have been that bad. Sometimes the initial romance blinds people to certain things that the harsh realities of married life often bring to the fore. Still, all may not be lost; and you may be more attuned to each other than you realize.
10. **You fight the "wrong" way:** If you can't focus on the topic of your argument, opting instead to bring up past mistakes or reopen old wounds, then your marriage may be leaning towards "over." The more past conflicts come into current arguments, the less healthy your marriage is.

11. **Improve your marriage:** It is not necessary to consider marriage counseling only in case of problems. Sometimes, it pays to seek marriage counseling just to enrich the quality of a marriage. Being proactive can pay rich dividends and bring a new awareness of each other's significance in the relationship.

Whatever reason is that motivates you to seek marriage counseling, remember it has to be with the mutual agreement and cooperation of both partners. For counseling to be *truly successful* in *improving* a marriage or relationship, each partner must undertake counseling sessions with an open mind and a true heart.

Chapter Twenty-Four

If you can't have a happy marriage, at least have a happy divorce.

If you have kids you never *really* get divorced. There will be a connection between the two of you through them for the rest of your lives. Divorce often carries the same emotional weight for children as a death in the family or an unexpected relocation. Preparing a child for the realities of a divorce is never going to be an easy process for any parent. The fear of causing permanent emotional scars or of alienating a child for life are very legitimate fears. Both parents need to be in agreement as to what will be said, before having *any talks* about divorce with their *children*.

One of the most important ways to prepare your child for divorce is to make sure you're prepared first.

Divorce is stressful for parents and kids alike. Although the reactions of your children will depend on age, temperament, and the circumstances surrounding the split, many kids feel sad, frustrated, angry, and anxious. It is not uncommon for them to 'act out' *because* of those feelings. Marriage counselors can help provide parents with straightforward advice on breaking the news to younger children.

It's wrong to separate the children after a divorce.

Finders Keepers Losers Weepers

Many parents facing a divorce worry about the psychological and emotional damage their actions will cause to a child. The truth is, no matter how carefully you broach the subject or how many euphemisms you use, news of this magnitude is going to cause *some* emotional damage to children. *It can't be avoided.* The good news is that *most* children are *amazingly* resilient and *better* at coping than we think. Preparing your child for the first divorce discussion may simply be a matter of finding the right time and place.

One way to broach the subject of divorce with a child is to think on his or her age level.

Terms like legal separation, divorce, or custody may sound foreign to a younger child; but a five-year-old understands friendships and arguments and visits. You may want to explain that Mommy and Daddy are trying to be friends, but they need to live in different houses so they can stop arguing about things. Sometimes you'll get to visit Daddy, and sometimes you'll stay with Mommy. With younger kids, it's best to keep it simple. You might say something like. "Mom and dad are going to live in different houses so they don't fight so much, but we both love you very much and will try to help you get through this." Older kids and teens may be more in tune with what parents have been going through, and may be more probing — and difficult — they may ask questions about things based on what they've overheard and picked up on from conversations and fights.

Our divorce is not your fault.

As a parent, you'll need to reassure older children that the problems between Mom and Dad are not their fault. Apologize for anything a child might have accidentally overheard during a heated discussion. As painful as a divorce may be, witnessing more years of physical or emotional abuse can be even more damaging to a child.

It will not be like we used to live.

Finders Keepers Losers Weepers

Give kids enough information to prepare them for any upcoming changes in their lives. Try to answer their questions as truthfully as possible, in a way that they can understand and process. Remember that kids don't need to know every last detail — they just need to know enough to understand clearly how their lives are going to change. Above all, be as honest with your child about your impending divorce as you can be. Explain the custodial terms in plain language: "You'll be living with me in this house for the school year, and Daddy will pick you up on Friday nights to stay at his house for the weekends. During the summer, you can stay at my house or Dad's house. Sometimes you'll have Christmas with me and sometimes you'll have Easter at Dad's house." Children often want to hear what will remain the same for them, such as school attendance and participation in sports or other interests.

Help them put their feelings into words.

Children's behavior can often clue you in to their feelings of sadness or anger. Let them voice their emotions and help them to label them without trying to change their emotions or explain them away. You might say, "It seems as if you're feeling sad right now. Do you know what's making you feel so sad?" Be a good listener when they respond, even if it's difficult for you to hear what they have to say.

Your kids come first.

Whatever arrangement you choose, your child's needs should always come first. Avoid getting involved in a tug of war as a way to "win." When deciding how to handle holidays, birthdays, and vacations, stay focused on what's best for the kids. It's important for parents to resolve these issues themselves and not ask the kids to choose.

Get help dealing with your own painful feelings about the divorce.

If you're able to adjust, your kids will be more likely adjust. Also, getting needed emotional support and being able to air your feelings and thoughts with an adult will lessen the possibility of your child shouldering the unfair burden of your emotional concerns. Confidants may include trusted friends, family members or therapists.

Be patient with yourself and with your child.

Emotional concerns, loss, and hurt following divorce take time to heal, and this often happens in phases. That's healthy. Recognize the signs of stress. Consult your child's teacher, doctor, or a child therapist for guidance on how to handle specific problems about which you are concerned.

Should you stay in a marriage and make it work? Reasons not to get a divorce...

For the children

Staying in the marriage for your children's sake, is one of the prime reasons cited by couples who have considered divorce at some point or another. Children from broken homes tend to suffer from more self-esteem problems. Changes in sleeping and eating habits, expression of anger, loss of some skills previously acquired, nightmares, and exhibiting sadness and grieving because of the absence of one parent, can all present themselves. The child may even be aggressive and violent to the parent they blame for the divorce. They may withdraw from friends and favorite activities, exhibit strange behavior, use foul language, and feel angry and uncertain about their concepts of love, marriage and family.

Think about all of these things and really think about whether divorce is the only way out. Is there any option of working on your marriage and making it a happy one? If you can do this, you may be teaching your child an important lesson. That lesson is you don't have to quit. Sometimes, you can work through tough times and things will come out better. Sometimes, there is no other option except divorce or separation, and sometimes you may surprise yourself, get help and reach resolve.

For marriage itself

Your life before marriage is totally different from your life after marriage. Home is a different concept. You have good memories and bad ones. Marriage is a journey. Marriage is an institution. Marriage is hard work. Maybe you can be the couple that valued the institution of marriage and made it work, despite all odds. If there's anything worth fighting for, it's a relationship that once had promise and potential.

For your health

It is a proven fact that divorce is bad for your health, as any change in lifestyle can cause depression and anxiety along with physical ailments that are stress induced. A study published in The Journal of Health and Social Behavior, analyzed data from nearly 9,000 adults nationwide, ages 51 to 61, and found those who had been divorced or widowed suffered 20 percent more chronic health conditions, such as heart disease, diabetes or cancer, than individuals who were currently married.

For your Money

Finance is another aspect that makes people rethink divorce. Most people also put off a divorce, because of the insane expenditure involved. Legal fees, child support, alimony/palimony, different living arrangements, etc., can put a hole in your bank account. Married couples also tend to make more informed and less risky investment decisions. Additionally, when you're single, you tend to spend a month's salary on a dress or dip into your savings to take a vacation. With another person in the relationship, there is accountability, and you have to spend responsibly. People also start saving marriage, because of the natural progression of their lifestyle.

Life after divorce

When you get a divorce, you'll be out in the whole dating zone again. Although that seems exciting for some people, the whole process of dating can be daunting. There are a few things you'll never have to worry about after you're married. You'll never have to be on your guard and be on your best behavior to impress the other person. You can be yourself. You can burp and scratch when you want to. You do not need to worry if your hair is limp or if your clothes are creased.

If you have invested a lot of time and effort in the relationship, that is a good reason to rethink the divorce. You have spent years getting accustomed to your partner's way of life, likes, dislikes, habits, temperament, etc. Any other relationship or marriage will take as much time and effort as this one. Are things really so bad that you're willing to throw all this away to take your chance on another relationship that may or may not be the same? Chances of a second marriage ending in divorce are also quite likely, as most people subconsciously look for someone similar to their first spouse and will probably make the same mistakes in the marriage again.

CHAPTER TWENTY-FIVE

I'm a good woman and you're a good man. Are we a good match?

Sometimes when we love someone we don't have the courage to express our feelings, because we're not sure if the feelings are mutual. You can hide feelings, but sometimes feelings refuse to be hidden. What can you do to find out how the other person feels?

You can say "I love you" in a million ways that aren't verbal. And the beauty of *those* ways will have *more* effect than mere words. Expression has no boundaries. Feelings are always better expressed than said. A look, a smile, a touch, a gift, caring, etc. are all ways to show how you feel. However, you *do* have to choose a smart man (or woman) who understands the *true* language of love.

If you have been friends for a long time and now you want to be more than friends, your prospective love interest probably does not see you in that light. In this case, you must "change yourself" in the sense that you have to portray yourself as someone they can love and be attracted to, instead of just someone who enjoys spending time with them and vice versa. This change needs to be something positive for yourself and illustrate your good qualities. For example, start going to the gym, get in shape, or wear nice clothes. Suddenly, your friend starts seeing that well-toned person of their dreams with the personality they have loved all along.

Wait for the right moment. Don't express your feelings when you are among friends. Wait until you are alone. But when you are, don't wait. Respect the reaction to your proffer of love. If this person doesn't love you back, your life isn't finished. It may hurt, but that's how they feel. Don't make a big production out of it. Just give it to them straight. Acting like a drama king or queen could make them reject you. Don't get angry they say nothing. "I love you," is a statement, not a question. Don't expect an answer, because it doesn't exist. If you are rejected, ask if you can stay friends. Letting that person know you care about them might help change their mind later. Love can be a tricky thing

On the other hand, your friend may say he or she loves you back. Be prepared for that. If they do love you, don't pour out every single feeling you have for them right away. Express it over time, and savor the experience of love.

Does romance still exist?

Everyone has his own concept about love, but do you think if you were living 200 years ago you would have the same concept of love? Some will argue that even the ways to express love have changed. However, this is entirely untrue. For example, if you are a man did you know that many of the old ways used to express love will make your love interest much happier? A woman still loves love letters! Have you ever written a love letter to your partner? Have you ever sent an email or an early morning SMS full of romantic words or sent a romantic poem? Have you ever written a romantic poem for her even though you don't know how to write a poem? Did you know most women would *love* to be serenaded or that red roses and champagne work like magic? All women like red roses, champagne, chocolate and perfume; and when you ask someone to marry you, the classic mental image a woman holds in her heart is that of a man kneeling before her, asking the one he loves more than anything in the world for her hand in marriage.

The truth is *every woman* wishes that the one she loves will express his love in these amazing romantic, old-fashioned ways. If you want to keep romance alive, all you have to do is look into your heart and into the past.

The more we love the person, the fewer flowers we use in the bouquet, until one flower is left.

If someone gives you a bunch of flowers, that person is a friend. If he gives you 2 flowers, he's pointing to himself and to you. It is an invitation to come closer. If he gives you a single flower, he's in love with you.

One of the best, and easiest, ways to bring a smile to a woman's face is to give her flowers. Once I read a brilliant idea for giving a flower to the woman you love.

Step 1: *Buy her a fresh bouquet of red roses.*
Step 2: *Buy a matching fake rose.*
Step 3: *Slide the fake rose into the bouquet of real roses.*
Step 4*: Tell her, "I will love you until the last rose dies."*
(She won't know what you did and she will think your being a nut for a while but it's worth it in the end.)
Step 5: *Don't tell her what you did! Let her find out on her own.*
(She will wonder why they all dried up and died and one lived, she'll remember what you said and before she notices its fake she'll think you pulled off a miracle.)

This is just one way to warm her heart. Doing hidden things like this is what I love about love.

Finders Keepers Losers Weepers

Also remember that a red rose given on an ordinary day, is worth million red roses on Valentine Day.

Online Relationships

Every minute of every day at least one new online relationship starts. We cannot ignore this kind of relationship. Who doesn't know at least ten couples who met through the internet? Everywhere around the world online dating is becoming more and more prevalent and acceptable and people are becoming more and more comfortable using computers as a means of instant communication. Email, instant messaging, and other applications like Facebook and Twitter, have all increased the comfort level and frequency of communication with family, relatives, and friends online.

Do you believe that an online relationship can lead to a happy marriage? Do you believe you will find your one and only in one of these chat rooms? Will you merely end up in love with a screen and a keyboard? Can the relationship possibly be a real one, or will it just be a text relationship? After all, the voice you hear when you type is your own voice. Are web cams really enough to get to know your partner face to face?

A survey was conducted on the question, "Do you believe in love through Internet?" The sample was 202 adults. The result was 49% affirmative responses and 51% negative responses.

Well, there is no a stable rule in these relationships. Let me explain something. Sometimes these kinds of relationships provide you an option to see your partner with your heart before you see that person with your eyes. You might think you can know everything about a person, because you can live with this person 24/7 on the internet if you do nothing but sit at your computer. On the other hand, sometimes you just know your idea about the person in front of the other screen. There are invisible modes, block persons, fake accounts, fake photos, etc. All of these things exist in this life. Online life is different from the world of real life. When you meet your on line love in real life there are two options that will confront you. 1) You may sit with that person for ten minutes and find out who that person is and discover they not the same person you chatted with on line for the last month; or 2) You might say "Oh, last I'm with you."

You know that an online relationship has worth when your online partner:

1. Is eager to get together with you as much as possible in person after a reasonable amount of time (when you both feel ready and comfortable.)
2. Stops browsing the dating sites for other people after meeting you. If you are looking for serious love and the person claims to really like you and is truly interested in forming a relationship with you, then they will no longer feel the need to explore "other fish in the sea."

One more major thing you must always remember to stay in touch with is your instincts. Many people ignore their instincts, telling themselves that they are just being paranoid or picky. They'd rather ignore red flags instead of faces the truth because they so want to believe that they have found true love. Do yourself a favor and trust that inner voice inside you---your best friend who will never lie to you. Do not lower your standards, and *never* settle for less out of fear of being alone.

Real life relationships vs. online relationships

1. For some people, online relationships encourage more self-expression and self-reflection than real life communication and for others, less.
2. Some people experience online relationships as more predictable, safe, and less anxiety-provoking than real life relationships.
3. People who are very verbal and expressive offline may not be in an online relationship and vice versa.

4. People who lack face to face verbal skills may prefer online relationships.
5. Some important aspects of a person may be obvious in person, but almost invisible online.
6. Some people prefer the online relationship over knowing each other in real life.
7. Elements of people's online relationships may reveal what's missing in their real life relationships.
8. In online relationships, some people explore their interpersonal style and experiment with new behaviors. What is learned online can be carried into offline relationships.
9. Online relationships form and disappear more easily than real life relationships.
10. Intimacy develops more rapidly in online relationships than in real life relationships.
11. Combining real life contact with online contact of various types offers people the opportunity to explore and integrate different cognitive styles and ways of being. Different channels of communication may work best for different people.
12. Close online relationships naturally progress to real life meetings.
13. Meeting face to face for the first time changes how one subsequently perceives the other online.
14. Meeting face to face enriches the online relationship and/or challenges the image one had of the online other.
15. Interacting with someone online and offline on an ongoing basis may result in a "separate tracks" relationship. The relationship may be a bit different online than it is offline.

Remember, that long distance relationships work only if you're serious about it. If you're committed and you really love them and know they're coming back, then it'll work.

Marriage is a relation-ship, not a relation-boat.

Give it space to grow.

However much you love your work, you still need a vacation. However much you love your family, you still need some time alone. When couples dedicate themselves to allowing each other the space and outside interests they need, they have stronger marriages. In the words of Lebanese poet and philosopher Khalil Gibran, "Sing and dance together and be joyous, but let each of you be alone." He recognized that in order for a marriage to be joyous, the individuals within it must remain individuals. Bond with your spouse, but don't lose yourself within that bond. Two wholes are always stronger than two halves.

Recommendations when discussing your need for space

- Define what type of space you need and be honest. Talk openly with your partner. Tell him or her why you need space, and what kind of space you need, quiet space, working space, emotional space, fun space, away space, financial space.

- Be very clear about the need for space, and why you feel you need it. Discuss terms, so that he understands. Even if you think it is about him, it really is about you, so you are not allowed to make it about him. If you really think it is about issues he has, then break-up and move on with your life.

- Don't wait until you are feeling suffocated or trapped in your marriage to ask for space.

- Accept that wanting or needing space in your marriage is okay. It doesn't mean that your marriage is in trouble.

- Do not use your request for space as a test of him. If you ask for space to work on your feelings, self, or whatever, it does not mean he owes you any less faithfulness. Hopefully, he won't go out with your best friend or another woman, but you cannot throw up his seeing other people as a reason to later break up with him if this has been encompassed in the parameters you have set. If you have not decided separate, legally or otherwise, that is different.

- ☐ If you are married, let your spouse know that you are still very committed to your marriage, and that you needing space or alone time or away time doesn't diminish your love or desire for him or her.

- ☐ If your spouse is asking for some space, don't take it personally; and also don't measure or judge your marriage by the way other couples live. Do what is best for the both of you.

Keep your mood 'remote control' with you.
Control yourself and do not make others do that for you.

Many of us learned to believe early in life that other people determine our happiness. We might learn to live by this belief before we learn to talk or walk. This is the first false belief we create about our relationships. We can find a clue to this in our subconscious behind comments we make such as, "He makes me so happy." The truth is that you make yourself happy.

The first step in finding happiness is to understand that happiness always comes from inside you. Even if your experience of happiness appears to be coming from an outer source or experience, the actual happiness is coming from within you.

You can be happy while enjoying whatever role you are playing - flowing and growing while being whoever you are, however you are, and wherever you are. Some people may even find happiness in being somewhat of a curmudgeon. In fact, quite a few journalists and media personalities have made fortunes from doing just that!

Just imagine what it would feel like to simply accept and believe that you are already, always, automatically, deeply and profoundly happy, and to know that you will always inherently be happy, regardless of what does or doesn't happen in your life.

Finders Keepers Losers Weepers

Remember, Happiness starts inside of you and then radiates out to the things that you do. I often tell others there is nothing in the world outside of you that can make you happy or sad. This means you choose each moment of each day and how you will respond to your life. You have the ability to choose happiness over negative emotions. You have the ability to choose happiness and peace instead of anguish. Give it a try. Choose happiness.

We are not powerless. We have ability to master our emotions. That includes choosing happiness. You have nothing to lose and everything to gain. Give happiness a try. Unlock the happiness inside you.

Chapter Twenty-Six

Why do Single women like married men?

No long-term commitment

Single women who date married men often do so because they know the affair does not come with expectations of long-term commitments. This frees the woman to have a good time without having to look ahead or succumb to the pressures of a long-term relationship. She may find that she is having a swell time with her job, partner and friends and may not feel the need to get married or have kids. If her partner is a single man, he may feel otherwise and wish to cement their relationship into something more permanent. A married man, on the other hand, is already committed to another woman and is certain to have no such expectations from his single lady friend.

If you're not looking for a commitment why choose someone who is supposed to be committed for life? Why not a single guy? How easy can it be to be in a relationship with a married man? There is no way you can say it's only something to do from time to time. Feelings have to be factored into life equations. Recognize you didn't like him because he was easy. Something about him drew you to him in the first place.

'Mate-copying'

A study conducted by the University of Louisville found single women often indulged in a phenomenon known as "mate copying." According to this study, a single woman may be attracted to a married man because she feels if another smart and good-looking woman has already chosen this man, he must be special in some way.

The sense of competition

Women with a strong competitive streak may also be attracted to married men. Such a woman may be willing to take a married man as a lover to prove she is superior to the wife when it comes having the goods that attract men. She may hear her lover praise his wife and then be goaded to better her in the same or in another aspect. The phenomenon may have little or nothing to do with the desirability of the man in question, but just the fact he has transgressed on his marriage to be with her, is a huge ego trip.

More fun

Very often the attraction a single woman feels for her married lover is really the excitement of doing something immoral. If the woman is a rule-breaker at heart, she may set out to tempt a married man into a relationship simply because it is more fun doing what you are *not* supposed to do.

Wanting what you can't have

Contemporary society is hugely permissive when it comes to sexual relationships between partners who are not yet married. But the relationship between a single woman and a married man is still not open to social sanction. This may make the relationship that much more appealing for a single woman. She may find the whole routine of being secretive, going for clandestine meetings and experiencing quick sexual episodes, a huge turn-on compared to the much tamer relationship with a single man.

Married men in general

Many women feel that a married man, in comparison to a bachelor, can meet her emotional or material needs in a better manner, and have the answers to all her problems, as he is more experienced in handling these issues. Some women feel married men with a lot of sexual experience are a better catch than a bachelor who may be inexperienced in sex. For some, a married man is someone with whom they can indulge in fantasies and give them a great time

Playing out a fantasy

Very often the fantasy element is the key to the attraction between a single woman and a married man. The woman is drunk with the fantasy of her power because she has compelled an attached man to cheat on his wife. The man can live out sexual fantasies his wife refused him. This mutual fantasy life, however, begins to fall apart once the pulls and pressures of a normal relationship creep into the fantasy. If they begin to live together, they are likely to find the fantasy fizzling. Jealousies and insecurities ruin what they once shared.

Freedom

Single women who date attached men like the breathing space they get in the relationship. There is no one to answer to if she decides to catch a movie with a male friend or if she wants to go over old times with a former lover. The male partner who is already cheating on his wife is hardly in a position to get jealous or possessive with his lover and knows the moment he does, she would probably walk out.

Love

Finders Keepers Losers Weepers

Love can happen to anyone. As the popular saying goes, 'Love is blind'. When someone is in love the fact the object of love is already married is not going to matter much.

Do not waste your time in a useless relationship. All you end up with a broken heart. Think with your head and not your heart when it comes to a married man..

Chapter Twenty-Seven

Being ignored hurts more than hate.

Love and hate are like black and white.

When someone ignores you, especially if you love them, it is worse than if they hate you. Unhealthy relationships start with ignoring red flags.

Why is he ignoring you?

Your guy may be ignoring you and your relationship for a variety of reasons. Below are the most common reasons, and what you can do to get his attention.

- **He may be bored**. Your guy may be bored from the daily grind of not only) your relationship, but (also) his job, his family or his friends. He may be looking for a little adventure, and you're just the person to give it to him. Schedule some one-on-one fun with your guy to get him out of his rut.
- **He may be unhappy.** You might have a more serious problem on your hands if your guy is unhappy in an area of his life. He might be unhappy with his boss, a friend or a family member.

If that's the case, you've got to sit your guy down and talk it out. Get to the root of his unhappy feelings, and work out a plan together to fix it.

- **He may be sad.** Something's got your guy down. He may have had a setback at work that he's not sharing with you. He may not be feeling well and can't figure out why. There are countless reasons why your guy may be sporting a long face, but it's up to you to help him get happy again. Take him out for a fun night on the town and find out what's really making him sad. Offer to work together to get him back on track. He'll love you for it!

Showing Her You Care:

Show your love. Everyone loves to be loved, and woman loves to be pampered. Even if you have a steady girlfriend, it is necessary to give her some part of your day. You should talk to her at least twice a day.

Don't talk about your past love life. There is no need to check out other girls in her presence. Pick her up and drop her at her doorstep and say something nice. When you go out with her let her feel that she is the only person there. Call her in the middle of her day and take her out for coffee after work. Send her an SMS just to tell her how much you miss her. Don't forget to compliment her and tell her she's as beautiful as first day you met. It's good to hear that you still like how she looks.

Be sensitive and carrying: Ask her if is something wrong if you see she is upset. Listen to her and try to make her smile again. Remind her that her problems are your problems, and you want to share all problems in life together.

Remember your anniversary and her birthday. A woman nearly always knows these dates. That's why she'll be impressed and *very* happy to see you are *a caring man* who remembers these important dates, even if *she* forgets them.

Prepare her a romantic weekend she doesn't expect. Spend a romantic weekend away with your partner where nobody can reach and disturb you. It's a perfect opportunity to reignite the love between you.

Once you begin to pay attention to what brings her pleasure and happiness, you're on your way to being a true romantic. The thing to keep in mind is that romance is about *her* desires, *not yours*. Your satisfaction comes from her joy.

Chapter Twenty-Eight

When I said hello, he said good-by.
When I said good-by, he said hello.
In Both cases it was good-by.

I don't like a man or woman who treats a partner like a yoyo. This happens when your partner doesn't feel secure in your relationship and cannot decide if whether to stay in relationship or to let it go.

Even the strongest among us needs to feel secure.

In the course of a relationship, trust and a sense of security play a major role in determining the direction of the relationship. Without security, any relationship will fall apart. Healthy couples require a feeling of security in their relationships, and it is impossible to maintain a relationship without trust.

Signs your partner overly insecure

1. **Extreme jealousy**: If your partner is confident about his or her physical appearance and your attraction them, then they shouldn't feel threatened by the presence of another, especially if that person is your cousin, friend, sister, or mother.

Finders Keepers Losers Weepers

2. **He or she is a snoop**: Your partner wants access to every personal detail of your life. They go through your voice mail, reads your e-mail, and ask your friends personal questions about you when you're not around.

3. **Constant state of paranoia:** Anything you do causes them to become suspicious and prompts questions. "Why are you going to the gym? Why did you get a haircut? Why did you buy new underwear? Why did you shave? Why did you brush your teeth? Why are you taking a shower? Why are you so happy? Do you still love me? Why are you breathing?" You get the point.

4. **Your partner requires daily reports:** They expect you to call r every hour of the day, and if you forget or miss a call, you'll have a lot of explaining to do.

5. **Low self-esteem:** Low self-esteem can have a detrimental affect on a relationship if one partner depends on the other to maintain their self-image, or to validate their opinions..

Ways to improve your sense of security in a relationship:

1. **Be secure with yourself:** To be secure in any relationship you must be secure with yourself and who you are as a person. If you are without self-confidence and self- esteem, you may be insecure about both your personal relationships and relationships with other people. You will have difficulty standing up for yourself if you do not have to self-esteem. You must speak up and be secure in what you are bringing to amy relationship.
2. **Good communication**: The first step to having security in any relationship is to build healthy communication between you. Both you and your partner must feel safe enough to tell one another how you and think and feel about the relationship. You

need to listen, understand, and affirm your partner's feelings and vice-versa. This means that and your partner must learn to identify, label and communicate your feelings effectively to each other.

3. **Understand your partner**: This the best way to improve the sense of security in your relationship. Try to understand your partner's feelings and views. Everyone has different expectations about what it means to feel secure in a relationship due to past experiences with other relationships. It is important to realize this in order to maintain a mutual understanding and sense of security. Discuss these things with your partner with open heart. The best way to be trusted is to be truthful to yourself and as well as to your partner.

4. **Refrain from pre-judgment:** In the course of your relationship, there will be times when you do not understand your partner and why they acted the way they did and/or why they feel certain that you cannot comprehend what has been done. It is important that you stay calm. These feelings are completely normal in a relationship. When this happens, you must refrain from pre-judging the event. Do not tell your partner he or she is crazy, stupid etc. This will indirectly break the sense of security your partner has in the relationship. Support this temporary behavior by affirmation, and encourage them to engage in expressing feeling, noting it is safe to do so.

5. **Support each other emotionally:** The most important security factor in a relationship is the ability of the couple to provide emotional support to one another. Learning to read or identifying your partner's emotional level at any given point of time is the first step to emotional support. The next step is learning to give the appropriate emotional response the moment you detect changes in your partner. The ability to

Finders Keepers Losers Weepers

detect and support your partner's emotional state will make a big difference in your trust relationship..

Chapter Twenty-Nine

When a man cheats on his wife he breaks her heart. When woman cheats on her husband she breaks him.

It has been estimated more than half of all husbands in the United States have had at least one extramarital affair. This is a grim statistic and a scary reality. .

Cheating is cheating and it doesn't matter if you are a man or a woman. It takes two people to cheat. It takes one person to cheat on and hurt or destroy another person. When a man cheats on a woman, he breaks her heart; but when woman cheats on a man she breaks his soul. We all have intuition. Whether you call it a "sixth sense," "warning bells," or "red flags." Trust that inner voice. Unless you are a generally suspicious person and have a history of being overly possessive and accusing, your fears are probably justified.

Signs your spouse may be cheating:

1. **Your spouse is making excuses.** "Sorry, I've got to work late again, dear. Sorry, my friend has a problem. Sorry I must travel. They asked me to do that at work. . ." *Suddenly,* your husband or wife is gone *a lot more often!* There may be excuses, but they *don't* have a ring of truth. The time away seems excessive, and unusual. Logistically, your spouse can't

be unfaithful while they are with you at home. The more time they are away, the greater the opportunity is to cheat.

2. **Mirror, mirror on the wall:** Your spouse is becoming preoccupied with his or her appearance. I think this is a *very big* indicator your partner may be cheating. Remember how you acted when you first met and dated your spouse? You got spiffed up, got some new clothes, went to the gym, and got a tan. You will also see these behaviors in an unfaithful spouse.

3. **A very shallow communication:** Your spouse doesn't speak to you about personal feelings. The communication between the two of you is very shallow--just business talk and stuff about the kids. Not only that, but your spouse seems aloof, detached, and even irritable. He might pick fights for no apparent reason, or she might not care about family vacations, fixing up the house, or other domestic responsibilities.

4. **New cell phone unknown number:** Your spouse may get a new cell phone, or maybe you don't see your spouse's cell phone bill anymore. Perhaps you discover a number repeated numerous times at odd hours, and when you ask them they said it is an "opposite sex good friend." It also appears while their friendship is strong, you and your spouse are less friendly.

5. **You can't get your spouse interested:** You're hearing "I'm too tired," or "I've got a headache," night after night. You feel rejected and abandoned. Perhaps your spouse wants to do strange things in the bedroom that make you uncomfortable, and if you refuse to do these things, he just leaves you alone to sleep through the night.

6. **I think he is not honest with me:** You've caught your spouse in a lie, or in several lies, about his whereabouts and/ or

activities. Something he's told you doesn't make sense, but you can't quite pinpoint why!

How do you respond to your spouse being unfaithful? Take your time, and make no immediate decisions.

Marriage is a lifetime decision. When we make it we must accept it as it is. Any marriage will have its ups and its downs. marriage is a challenge. It is not about just you and your partner. There are a lot of things, people, and events to consider. You must think about all of that before you make any decision to get married, especially if the new marriage will end your current marriage. And if you can't reconcile the fact your spouse has been unfaithful and continue in the marriage and forgive him and you decide to end the marriage, you must still think about everything and everyone, and be sure of your decision, especially if there are children involved.

Accept your feelings:

Whatever you feel, anger, shock, uncertainty, agitation, fear, pain, depression, or confusion or a combination of one or all of these things, remember that it is normal to feel like this. Tears are healthy. It is okay to cry.

Share a community:

There are websites that allow you to write and express your thoughts, and you will find a lot of individuals who can help you to get over and what you feel.

Stop blaming yourself:

You are not the reason your spouse cheated! Stop looking for a reason for the cheating, because there is no reason for cheating, there are just justifications that are not true. There is no simple answer to why someone becomes unfaithful. It could be a symptom of other problems in the marriage or it could relate to something in your spouse's past. You may never know why.

Chapter Thirty
Having sex with a man who is not your husband!

Your body is God gift. Don't abuse your body by having sex with someone who is not your husband. Don't deceive yourself. once you have sex with a man who is not your husband, he may never admit it, but he has lost a degree of respect for you. If you don't believe this, ask any honorable man or virtuous woman. If a woman was sleeping with *your* husband, wouldn't *you* think she was doing something wrong? How would you feel? If you want to have sex, have sex with your husband. If your sexual life with your husband is in the pits, to talk to him. Find some games to enrich your sexual life. If you are still not happy consider obtaining relationship counseling. If that doesn't work, leave him. It is better than cheating.

Respect your body. You are not a car. If you meet a man who wants to give you a test drive, send him to a car dealership. Bid him adieu and don't look back.

There is a vast difference between sex and love. Most men know the difference, and you had better learn it fast! If you fail or refuse to do so, you are surely headed for a doomed relationship or marital crash and burn.

Even if you don't touch another person, you can still cheat on your partner with cybersex.

Finders Keepers Losers Weepers

Exactly what is cybersex? Cybersex is a combination of communication and masturbation. It is a selfish gratification of one's sexual desires while sharing one's most intimate thoughts and fantasies with someone else experiences online via text or multimedia.

Cybersex has become the easiest way to cheat on your spouse. In the past it was hard to get sex. You had to sneak around and really look for it. Now it is easy. Cybersex brings it right into the house, Cybersex is also easier to hide, and it usually doesn't cost money.

The big question here is "Is cybersex cheating?" Before you answer this question, ask yourself how you would feel if you found your partner, mate or date doing what you are doing? If you would be hurt, upset and feel betrayed, then the answer is you're cheating, and never try to convince yourself otherwise.

Let me explain my point. Internet is a tool. It is not life. Don't waste your real life for a fake life. People who have online affairs imagine they are in love with people they have never met in person. They spend hours talking to them online, they exchange pictures, and they send flowers and gifts. They even leave their spouses for people they have never met.

The only real difference between cybersex and "real" sex is physical presence. When you enter into a marriage, it is you and another person promising to stay faithful and to be with just you for the rest of your lives.

I can vouch for the fact that cybersex makes the other person feel worthless, and violated, and that it turns into an emotional rollercoaster. If you are not okay being in a monogamous, respectful, trusting relationship, then why did you get married or commit yourself to another person? There is a major difference between porn and cybersex. Porn is just watched and has no attachment. When you are cybering you control the situation and go where you want to go. This is personal. It is cheating because it involves emotional attachment, especially when you are doing it with the same person over and over again.

Yes, there's no real connection; but there is a real person on the other end. If emotions are involved, it's cheating. If you are exchanging pictures and gifts, it's cheating. If there is a webcam, it's cheating. If it leads to talking on the phone or meeting, it's cheating. No matter how much you may want to delude yourself otherwise, having cybersex is just as much cheating on your mate as if you did the deed in person.

CHAPTER THIRTY-ONE
There are no reasons for cheating, only justifications.

Why do men cheat?

1. **Some men are only as faithful as their options.** Most men cheat because they had the option to cheat. The old saying 'men are only as faithful as their options' can sometimes ring true. Men don't get offered sex as often as women, so when the opportunity does arise, it can be very difficult for them to turn it down.

2. **Some men cheat because of their egos.** Cheating boosts their egos. Sometimes men don't feel like they are attractive to the opposite sex anymore, and when a woman shows some interest, not only does a man react, he may allow her to stroke his ego and more. There's nothing like the thrill of the chase to men on the hunt. When they are finally rewarded for their efforts, their egos swell even larger.

3. **Some men are looking for something in common.** You grow apart. Maybe the two of you didn't have as much in common as you thought. He's met a woman who has more in common with him who loves football or plays golf. He may see if he is compatible with her under the sheets as well.

4. **Some men cheat because you argue a lot.** Men will sometimes cheat to get away from an overly critical or argumentative partner. Who wants to be around someone who is constantly nagging or being critical?

5. **He has fallen out of love.** Sometimes men become so comfortable in a relationship, they don't know how to get out. They may be staying in the relationship because of children or financial reasons. However, they feel like they are missing out on love and may seek it elsewhere. In their minds, this is as close to a win-win as they can get.

6. **Your sex life sucks.** If a man has a disinterested partner or isn't getting enough sex to fulfill him, there is a good chance he will have an affair. Just because you have a husband or boyfriend, does not mean you can stop trying to please them. It takes a little bit of effort to keep your sex life from getting boring and non-existent. Some men cheat because they want to try new sexual things that their current partner will not try.

7. **Some men want revenge.** A man will sometimes cheat if he finds out his partner is or was cheating on him. How else is he supposed to heal those hurt feelings?

8. **It's new, different and exciting.** Some men get tired of having steak for dinner every night and want to try a hamburger. The same goes for sex with a woman. That's why men don't necessarily always cheat with women who are more attractive than their partners.

9. **They want to see if they can get away with it.** If a man has the attitude 'what she doesn't know, won't hurt her,' he may cheat to see if he is sneaky and smart enough to get away with

it. However, with all the advancement in surveillance and spy ware, getting caught has now become easier than ever.

10. **Once a cheater, always a cheater.** Because you have forgiven it in the past, he thinks he can do it again, If you have forgiven a cheating man a couple of times, they are more than likely going to cheat again, because they already know if they plead enough, you will forgive them.

Why women cheat

A woman's may get involved in an extra marital relation due to:

1. A powerful emotional and physical attraction of a colleague or other associate pulls the mind and heart to submit.
2. Dissatisfaction and boring emotional and physical relation with spouse leads to an extra marital relation.
3. There is a lack of motivation for deep involvement in home activities.
4. A fading spouse's sexual attraction is a step to establish an extra marital relationship.
5. For woman it is also revenge against the spouse when she is in a cruel or abusive relationship.
6. Genetic characteristics of individual for emotional and sexual desire for more sex, variety, addiction, curiosity, drawing opposite sex's attention to become special may play a factor.
7. She is too open minded and says, "I do not mind having extra-marital sex as we now live in a modern society."
8. She exhibits weak and submissive behaviour and submits to another's intentions.

Even though they say woman needs a reason to cheat and a man just needs a woman to cheat, To cheat you need two people. Some individuals are more prone to cheating than others.

Cheating just for the adventure:

Believe it or not there are some women who cheat just for the adventure and the sheer high they get from it. This kind of woman usually craves the variety and excitement of one-night stands or short-term affairs. She gets easily bored with the routine and the predictable and loves to live life a little dangerously. That includes seeking a little loving on the side.

The innermost desires:

There are some women who just aren't content with the physical side of their relationships. They are never satisfied with their sex lives. In some cases their partners fail to show enough interest in them. Either way they are left wanting. And this drives them into other men's arms in an effort to seek pleasure and satisfy their innermost desires.

What is good for the goose is good for the gander:

The woman who knows she's being cheated upon and in her hurt and anger she feels it is payback time. And so she decides to hit back in the same measure. Having done that, she realizes it's not so bad after all and figures two can play the same game.

Cheating for cheating:

And then there's the woman for whom cheating is an addiction as sure as others are addicted to alcohol. By cheating, she reassures herself she is still attractive and men find her desirable. Perhaps she has had an insecure or unpleasant childhood, or an early adulthood which has left its mark on her. As a result she finds it hard to commit to a relationship and to trust her instincts. By cheating, she knows where she is, and she is in control of the situation, keeping her emotions intact.

The unfulfilled woman:

This woman is deeply dissatisfied with her current relationship. She is either deprived of attention from her current partner, or is being neglected and needs to be reassured of her feminine attributes. She may be just plain lonely and need to be held, which often leads to intimacy and an affair.

The difference between "cheat" and "chat" is the letter "e"

Just like an alcoholic or a substance abuser starts with a few drinks or a trial experiment, chatting and emails lead to exchange of photographs, calls and finally meetings. And very soon it has become a full-blown affair. Internet infidelity has crossed geographical boundaries where those involved have been willing to negotiate distances and contend with secret meetings without their spouses' knowledge to take the relationship one step further.

It is natural for people to want to connect with other people. Flirting is also a natural, confidence-boosting activity that most people engage in without even realizing it. Not all Internet relationships are necessarily bad. The key is to draw a line in the sand. The location of this line will vary from couple to couple. Some people do not mind if their partners flirt or have friendships with people of the opposite sex, so long as the relationships never become physical or too time-consuming. Couples should talk to each other openly and decide what they feel comfortable with in this regard. In general, it is better to be safe than sorry, and people should avoid Internet relationships they think might hurt their partners if discovered.

Internet cheating can be very hurtful. If someone is spending a lot of time online and neglects their partner, then this will damage the relationship and can be considered cheating even if no physical contact is ever made. If it is discovered pictures were exchanged and sexual conversations were had, the cheating person's partner will be especially hurt and may feel undesired. Internet relationships are often discovered accidentally through emails and saved pictures, so no one should think that they are likely to get away with an online relationship. In the end, Internet cheating is a slippery slope, and even people who never meant to cause any harm might end up having a full-blown affair and are likely to get caught.

Chapter Thirty-Two

A woman unhappy in her relationship can't do well at work. A man unhappy at work can't do well in his relationship.

A woman unhappy in her relationship doesn't do well, not only at work but in her entire life. It will affect everything--work, friends, communication, going out, talking, smiling, even her health. Of course we can't generalize any issue such as this. Basically, this rule applies 70-80% of women based on psychological studies, meaning 20-30% of all women would normally need to be satisfied in their personal relationships to do well at work. To me personally, it never mattered. Sometimes a troubled personal relationship can provoke me (personally) to focus more on work. Everyone and every woman and every relationship is different.

Although you usually develop your relationship and your career separately, we all know through experience that they are connected. The quality of your love life will affect your work. If you're feeling stressed about your relationship, you will be on edge at work and will be less productive. If you're feeling great about your partner, you will sail through your day at work.

The opposite is also true. How your work is going will affect your relationship. This shouldn't be surprising, because most people spend more time at work than they spend awake with their spouses! If you are happy with your work, this will enhance your relationship. You will probably be in a good mood when you get home. You will be relatively relaxed and will have an enjoyable evening with your spouse. On the other hand, if your job is sheer drudgery, you will probably be stressed when you get home from work. You might spend your evening in a bad mood and complain about work.

> ***Those ridiculing love only made it through life because they were loved during their upbringings. Those ridiculing sex only exist as a result of it.***

Which is more important, sex or love? Many people pay more attention only to one side of this equation, and that's very common. There are two kinds of people. One pays attention to love and the other group pays attention to sex. Ridicule is an unnecessary option.

Love and sex are not the same thing. Love is an emotion or a feeling. There is no one definition of love because the word "love" can mean many different things to many different people. Sex, on the other hand, is a biological event. Even though there are different kinds of sex, most sexual acts have certain things in common. Sex may or may not include penetration. There is no exactly "right" definition of love. It is different for everybody. Love involves feelings of romance and/or attraction. Sex is an event or act (physical). There are different kinds of sex, but all kinds of sex have some things in common. The act of having sex can have nothing or everything to do with love. When it happens with love, it's a great way to show and share love, to create more love, and to make love stronger. Sex is something natural that feels great and can heal you emotionally and physically.

Personally, I don't know how my life would be without love, romantic love, love for my parents, friends, my future children, my future spouse. Love is a wonderful feeling. It is really good to love and be loved. Love is everything. I have seen people who are deeply in love, and they don't touch each other. This is what love is. Sex is a part of love, but love is not sex. I could live my whole life without having sex with the person I really love. Love is the precious gift given by God to mankind. On the other hand, sex gave you the life you live. If there was no sex we would never know new life, and we would never hear a baby cry. Life comes from sex as well as love.

It is not making love. It is showing love.
Love cannot be made!

Love cannot be made. We show love. Love can never be made. It is an incorrect phrase used to describe having sex. Love is felt, demonstrated, given, received, shared and followed. It has no physical existence. It has only emotional value. Love cannot be made. Love can only be shared and sex should be about love. When a couple expresses their love physically, and this results in the birth of a child, there is no better way to describe the result than "they showed love." This new human is pure love, made from showing love and sharing love. I know it sounds weird when you say to your husband "let's show love" instead of saying "let's make love." Perhaps it's the culture in which we live, howver to say we are making love doesn't begin to describe what transpires when two people who truly love each other become one with the act of sex.

When having sex is only about the act itself, I would call that merely sex. and when it's about the person and the act is just an extension of that. I'd call that making love. But when it's about two people expressing their love, that's when I'd call it showing love.

The older we become, the harder it is to choose a life partner and the easier it is to find friends.

Diedre said: "Today I feel a little bit lost. I am 32 years old. I recently lost my job because of the bad world crisis. I speak Turkish

English and German. I have a BA degree, and I am single do not see anyone. I am recovering from drug abuse. I have been clean for 5 years. My loving ex boyfriend got married and forgot about me. I feel lost as I have problems trusting anyone new. After my ex I only did drugs to get over my heartbreak. Now when I look back or to the future I think I lost my faith and wisdom. I think I need a close friend right now to cry their shoulder."

Well look at this? She said she wanted a friend! She didn't mention anything about being in a relationship.

Are you 38 and still single? And by single I mean never married. You ask yourself, "Why am I still single?" It's a question more than half of American women ask themselves, according to a report the New York Times printed in early 2007. This data includes women who live apart from their significant others, but all independent variables aside, it's a figure that's rocketed significantly in the last couple decades. There's a reason why you're 38 and single. Are you too focused on your career? Are you dating the wrong people? Are you ignoring issues that are getting in the way of being happy and secure? Figure it out and deal with it. All of that stuff comes from a place of fear, a fear that we will never meet anyone and that we will end up alone, a fear that we will be hurt or left or abandoned or that we won't be in control of the situation. Tell yourself that it will happen, and it will happen. But if you just sit counting the reasons why fate is against you, you're creating a big wall that will be very hard to scale. You have the ability to change your life and have the things you want. It all starts with you. You just have to truly want to change it. Stop focusing on what doesn't work and start focusing on what does work.

According to a recent study of happiness trends on Facebook, Deidre isn't alone. Research scientist Cameron Marlow analyzed millions of posts on the social networking site and discovered (among other things) that when women get engaged, they actually become less happy. Women can wait for 5 or 6 years just to get engaged; and even after dreaming and hoping for that proposal, when he finally pulls a ring out of his pocket and says, "Will you marry me?" even during the most romantic gondola ride in Italy, a woman might not say yes right away. Instead she may whisper, "Put that thing away," and half-seriously consider throwing herself overboard and into the murky water. After she says yes, she may even spend her entire engagement feeling anxious—and wondering if she made the right decision. Her self-doubt may make her question the relationship. Is she afraid she may say yes to the wrong person?

Here's the trouble: the more time we spend thinking about ourselves, formulating clever responses to friends' online comments about us, posting our most attractive photos, and "pimping our profiles" to leave impressions on our contacts, the less time we spend actually interacting with and caring about others.

Do not specify the Relationship between man and woman only in the space of admiration because it is not always like that.

The world is extremely mysterious. Every day we see many things that we take for granted without knowing how and why this happens. While "most people" see men and women sites on the Internet as a place to get together as a couple or in the physical or emotional sense, there are several types of relationships between men and women.

Friendship is found between the people having complementary thoughts. In the words of Mencius "Friendship is one mind in two bodies." The minds of males and females are as complementary as their bodies. Thus every man finds a different way of looking at the world, when he sees the worlds through the eyes of the woman. Thus a man who has good friendship with women is the epitome of "goodness" as his mind is fully grown up and mature. On the contrary, the people who do not have friends in the members of opposite sexes are truly evil without doubt, as their view is extremely unbalanced.

Dictators and despots never have friendships with women. This list includes Hitler, Stalin and Mao, who only had physical bonding with the women. Hence, their minds were never truly evolved. The mind of a person can have satisfaction, tranquility and peace only if it has friends in the members of the opposite sex.

Loving couples share the highest level of spiritual bonds with each other. The spiritual relationship is based on the non-physical relationship between the people. In this type of relationship, people have no expectation from each other as they all seems to merge their identity with God or the Holy Spirit that is the origin of all entities of the universe.

The spiritual or nonphysical bonding exists between people of opposite sexes in many forms. It is manifested in the form of love to mother, love to children, love to siblings and at later stage of life even between the love of spouses. Spiritual love is the final stage of love between every person when the bonding evolves to its highest level. The seed of this love is always present in the person, and it is first manifested in the child with his or her love of mother. Gradually, all other forms of love diminish and only the spiritual love remains in the most evolved human beings in this world . This form of love is truly selfless and unconditional.

Being friends with the opposite sex can be rewarding, and it can teach you how the opposite gender thinks.

Friendship between opposite sex people makes you know how other opposite sex thinks about you, maybe more than you know from marriage or another relationship.

1. **You must define your relationship as a friendship from the start.** In any relationship, cross-gender friendships included, communication is the key. Presumptions can lead to broken friendships, misunderstandings, and other problems down the

line. Egos aside, address why you both want to be just friends. There's a period in every opposite sex friendship that you question whether or not you should be more. Address it early on in the relationship. Both of you must want a strictly platonic friendship and understand that's all it will ever be. No matter what anyone says, it is possible to be just friends as long as you have that understanding (and a commitment to the friendship as just that) from the start.

2. **Don't give people a reason to think you're more than just friends**. Having a night out together is fine, but don't bring your friend into social scenarios where everyone else has a date. That is called dating, not friendship. You wouldn't ask your same sex friend to accompany you to your sister's wedding, so don't ask your opposite sex friend! If you are going somewhere that might appear romantic (e.g. a movie or a fancy restaurant) but you do not want it to appear that way, invite another friend of the same sex. Even then, people may insinuate that you are more than friends. Be prepared for those suggestions, and think of how you can deny them gracefully if this will be a problem to you. Otherwise, don't worry about what anyone will think, just know if you give off the wrong impression it may impede Mr. Right from stepping forward because Mr. Right will think your friend has taken the place he wants. You need to look available to be available.

3. **Don't be "touchy feely" with your friend.** Even if you consider yourself to be a naturally affectionate person, and especially if either of you are in a romantic relationship with someone else, keep our hands to yourselves. Sure, it's possible to make physical contact without inciting sexual attraction, but hormones can play tricks on us. Don't give those hormones a chance to confuse your status as friends. Limit hugs and physical contact to the same amount you share with a sibling or a co-worker, or same sex friend, depending on what you feel is appropriate, and what you think your significant other (or theirs) would feel

comfortable with in this area. If you find the need to hug and touch more, maybe you're not just friends.

What does it mean when woman changes her hair color?

When you look back at all the different reasons why you've changed your hair over the years, what would they be? A recent study explored that burning question. Commissioned by Andrew Collinge, a two-time winner of the prestigious British Hairdresser of the Year, the study found that the average woman changes her hairstyle a whopping 104 times in a lifetime. However, Collinge noted that these changes typically weren't all that dramatic. To find out the top 10 reasons why women switch up their coiffures, just read more.

Women Change their hair color and/or hairstyle. . .

1. Just for a change
2. Out of boredom
3. As a confidence booster
4. As a result of a breakup
5. To reinvent oneself
6. To keep up with fashions and trends
7. To cover gray
8. In conjunction with a milestone birthday
9. Either before or after having a child
10. Due to their wedding
11. Because it's the best way to cope

Changing your hair color after a big life change isn't crazy, but it might be the best way to cope. You break up with your long-term boyfriend and all of the sudden you can't stand your blonde hair. You're fired of your job so you decide to dye your hair red because that'll show your boss who is really is. It makes no real sense, but it helps you to cope when you make a change, any kind of change will do, and this change is simple and quick.

It's not unusual for a woman to want to do something for herself after a bad breakup. Be it going shopping or getting a pedicure. A woman needs, and should get some time on her own after splitting from her man – even psychologists know this and recommend it. Garnier Nutrisse also now reveals in a new study that this is not all that women do, since they also change hair colors in stressful moments. The recent survey shows that one in five women have changed hair colors in the aftermath of a life-altering event, and breaking up with a boyfriend is at the top of the list. Also, this is not just a subtle change we're talking about, as many women have admitted to going from one extreme to another, meaning, from blonde to black, and the other way around. The explanation for this can be multi-fold. Most of the time, it simply represented a woman's attempt to get back at her ex.

This is precisely why stylists are warning us to not give in to frustration and emotions, and to stop and reconsider any move we want to make before it's not too late. Other than changing hair colors, women also get what is known as a "post breakup haircut," which puts them at risk of being doubly miserable if things don't turn out well.

If you want to know a woman, steal her bag; and then you will know everything about her!

A purse defines a woman like blue jeans and T-Shirts define a man. The kinds of bags we choose, and their contents, can say a lot about our personality types. Three years ago someone stole my bag. I was crying. not just because I lost my bag, but because thief would know everything about my personal life. A bag's contents are different from woman to woman. Everything inside reveals a woman's personality. Women carry a lot of items in their purses, which are usually considered off limits to men due to the fact they often contain personal belongings a man might not want to see. Although possible, it is highly unlikely a woman is hiding something from her significant other in her bag.

"Forget looking into a woman's eyes - if you want to know her secrets, look inside her handbag." Yeah, if you stare at her eyes in order to tap her secrets just based on the saying that eyes are window of human heart, then you may seem a little out-of-date and disgusted. Just try to understand her through the things in her bag. You may wonder why, because they are common things used by ladies and nothing is special. So I will share with you some fresh things and insights into that mysterious bag.

1. There may be a random range of items in her bag, and it is often in chaos. You may guess she lacks order and is not good at arranging things. Actually, her handbag will evolve, bringing you surprise every time. Attention here: **she is creative**. An imaginative free spirit, hoarders have a creative nature and often try to rebel against conformity. Their bag is organized chaos and is like a bottomless pit. Everything from unpaid bills to food wrappers and change is mixed up and swimming inside. To the owner, the bag is packed full, yet functional; however, to the outsider this bag is chock-a-block. As her life is constantly evolving. She likes to swap her bag regularly to reflect her mood and match her outfit. She likes bright colored handbags including hot pink and aqua, revealing she is fun and approachable.
2. Anti-inflammatory pills to mints are included in her bag. And she loves to share her things with others. Some chocolates also can be seen in her handbag. Know what? She is thoughtful and know how to care about herself and others when out. Why? It's easy to know, for she prepares these things not just for herself, and she brings chocolate in case she or others she meet get hungry. **Maybe she is expressive.** Typically a reliable and detail-focused person, this bag is extremely organized, with a place and purpose for everything.

Finders Keepers Losers Weepers

She is very efficient and likes to be prepared for anything, carrying sensible items including hair accessories, tissues, toothbrush, hand wipes and even a phone charger. Although they are always on the go, they like the world around them to be structured, and therefore would rarely swap bags - their one favorite bag serves all purposes. They tend to choose neutral colored, classic cut handbags that will never go out of style.

3. She keeps everything neat and tidy in her handbag. She decreases the number of items in her bag to the minimum. To her, adding unnecessary things in her bag means additional weight. So, mind you here, she needs like things to be minimal and even people never verbose. Minimal is just ok. So if you say too much, just stop and let her enjoy some quiet time. **She is Minimal;** Logical and rational, these women hate clutter and like to keep their bag streamlined and neat. They are likely to carry a small bag that fits snugly underneath her shoulder, indicating class and sophistication. While she is always on the go, she only ever carries the necessities - usually just her wallet, sunglasses and an electronic organizer. She has mastered a system of organization, which means she'll never be stuck digging through receipts, food wrappers and bills to find her mobile phone!

Every woman has to be a man from 9:00 a.m. until 5:00 p.m. (Work time) and then a maid from 5:00 p.m. until bedtime

That is not always the case. In some marriages, men expect women to assume certain gender-stereotyped roles in managing a home for no other reason than because their mothers "always had a meal on the table" or "always ironed their father's shirts." One major difference today, however, is that in most marriages, the women are working the same or more hours outside of the home as the men are. This often leads to an imbalance of chores, stress, and burn-out among working wives, especially if these women are also mothers.

Finders Keepers Losers Weepers

Even in this day and age, women face discrimination and prejudice. Yet women all over the world continue to work hard to make a difference -- to alter their lives and the lives of others. And a woman may still try to act like a man at work, whether we like that or not. There are a lot of people who still tend to compare a man's and woman's work. And this is why we find that a woman will make an additional effort just to prove she can do the work of a man. As a defense mechanism, women have developed dual personas, one for the home and one for the workplace. Assuming a flirtatious and bubbly character at work results in wider acceptance among male workers, a woman may employ this as a means of getting along ay work, for example. This characteristic is independent of age and fairly present in today's male-oriented world.

Once she gets home her husband helps her, but she is still working! She has a lot of stuff on her plate. He has some stuff on his plate as well, yet it seems more often than not, the woman is the main work source at home. After she takes care of every detail of home, children, cooking, laundry, she can finally relax with her husband. She feels like a maid. However, not all women are maids, at least not in rich and developed countries; and in poor countries, rich people have maids, but women still face challenges.

Who plays with the cat, shouldn't mind its scratches.

Cats are tiny little women in fur coats. There are a lot of things that are common between women and cats, so I consider the above "Syrian Proverb" good advice you must remember when you deal with a woman. The difference between a dog and cat is, a dog thinks, "Hey, those people I live with feed me, love me, provide me with a nice, warm, dry house, pet me and take good care of me. They must be gods!" A cat thinks, "Hey, those people I live with feed me, love me, provide me with a nice, warm, dry house, pet me and take good care of me. I must be a god!" You can't discipline cats as you would dogs.

Finders Keepers Losers Weepers

No one owns a cat. No one owns a woman. Cats do what they want. They pout when they are not happy. They expect you to cater to their every whim. They're moody. They leave hair everywhere. They drive you nuts and cost you money.

The cat goes to the visitor who doesn't like cats more than to the visitor who likes cats! Usually, the person who doesn't like cats avoids looking at it, doesn't talk to it, and sits quietly, hoping to be ignored by the cat. The cat, therefore, sees the person's behavior as "cat-friendly" and practically inviting! If you notice women you will find some of them are like this. They attracted to men that avoid them more than those who stare at them!

A cat does a stiff-legged hop/touch against a human to say "hey, hi there, how ya doin'?" This is like a woman when they do one thing and mean something else.

A cat walks slowly, looking straight forward when passing another cat! This is what a woman does when staring at another woman. The fact is women look at other women more than men look to women. This occurs for two reasons. She either likes how the other woman is dressed, or she doesn't like her al all.

A cat frequently demands attention when you're on the telephone! The cat, since it can't see the person you are talking to, presumes you are talking to him and is responding to what he perceives is your conversation with him. I do that when my significant other is on the phone!

Facts about Women

- The last thing a woman wants to hear when she complains about her weight is a suggestion for a new diet plan.
- DON'T RELY ON INTUITION.

Finders Keepers Losers Weepers

- Women accumulate emotional wounds. Men accumulate disrespect wounds.
- A Man must use his own heart first to get to a woman's heart.
- Men and women are equals in duty, but their imagery is different.
- A Man often likes a woman impressed by him, not who impresses him.
- The first rule in getting along with women is to listen to them. The second rule is not to forget rule number one.
- The second rule to get along with men is give them appreciation. The first rule is "well known" which is actually the sex!
- If you are jealous, she says it's bad. If you don't get jealous, she thinks you don't love her.
- Women like to learn more than to be taught.
- You cannot expect a woman's reactions, and you cannot know a man's feelings.
- Sometimes a woman starts a fight with a man just because she's feeling ignored and wants to say, "Attention please!"
- I save all of your Voice mails and listen to them repeatedly, a secret every woman keeps from her man at the beginning of their relationship.
- Woman can destroy the relationship and never break up. The breaking up decision is usually made by the man.
- A man gets what he wants by acting smart, a woman by playing dumb.
- A woman wants to be cherished as child, treated as queen, and LOVED as a woman.

Chapter Thirty-Three

Women in love start to talk about wedding preparations and having a family.
She wants to get married BUT I DON'T!

When woman is really in love she talks of the future. Future plans, career, where she'd like to settle in, the number of cats in the house, even the color of the curtains --- these are all indications of a woman in love who is ready to tie the knot with the man of her dreams. Did she mention she loves breakfast in bed?

She talks about having kids. Kids can be a very sensitive topic and even newlyweds and couples married for years can have a hard time discussing this --- It depends on the priorities of the couple. of course. So when she does start to talk about this, there is no clearer sign she wants to get hitched. And she wants to make babies soon!

On the other hand, marriage is a big deal, one very sacred thing in a man's life --- it's when you say goodbye to your bachelor days, the flirting days, the hooking-up with lots of girl days and simply drowning into love and finally settling up with the girl you've been in love with all along. But you still cannot take this step.

Finders Keepers Losers Weepers

He said, "My girlfriend of two years is really pushing to get married. I think we're good like we are. I don't want to lose, her but I don't think I want to get married yet, or ever. I don't know. What should I do?"

Let's look at this closely. First of all, someone you're with for two years, that you would not even entertain the thought of marrying, deserves your honesty. You need to sit down with this chick and say it like you said it to me. You're happy with things the way they are. And you don't want to lose her. But you don't want to get married right now, and you aren't sure if that feeling is ever going to change. Talk about this with her. She should be someone that appreciates your honesty, candor, and willingness to have a conversation about this. She should hear you. She should respect that you have the right to feel the way you do, and she should appreciate you for who you are, not who she wants to change you into being. Doing this, you give her a chance to decide if she will continue in the relationship or not.

Women don't want to be married to anyone just for the sake of getting married. Women want to be married to the best man that they can find. Every woman has certain needs, and if she finds a man who can meet most of her needs, dreams and desires, then of course, she would never want to let him go. Women want to believe in something good. Women want to have close and caring relationships. If a woman wants to get married, then, of course, she wants to meet a man who wants to get married too. I don't think there is anything wrong with someone wanting to get married. I really don't. But I also see nothing wrong with not wanting to get married. What I see as wrong is not respecting your needs as well as respecting the needs of your partner. It's wrong when two people can't accept that they each want different things in life. She really can't expect to be able to pressure you into taking a huge life altering step that you don't want to take. But guess what, Skippy? It works both ways. The same goes for you. You can't expect her to give up on a huge life changing step that she wants to take.

Emotions vs. Respect

Men care more about respect, women about emotions; however, I know some women who also care about respect. Accumulated emotional wounds that lie deep inside are always brought to life when touched. I think both men and women are sensitive about the two wounds, but women can get over disrespect and can't get over the emotional factors, vice versa for men. It is the difference between women and men. Our nature is to segregate almost everything in an 'emotional' way, unlike men who are judging things through 'respect and honesty.' In ancient times it used to be 'classified' by saying women were loving and caring, and men were honest and brave.

A wound may be physical and psychological and the retention of a wound can also exist in both forms. To visualize this, you must realize that as far as the male is concerned, defeat is the most ignominy to a soldier. (Many even commit suicide.) He may also be wounded physically as a result. On the other hand, if a woman is physically abused by a male, she carries a wound that is emotional and a wound of disrespect. Similarly, a man physically abused by female, wounded in the disrespectful sense and as well as the emotional sense. There can be many hypotheses, but as I feel both male and female are prostrate and vulnerable to emotional and disrespect wounds that are derived from anyone, irrespective of gender.

Why is it always drama QUEEN (female)?
I would say there are plenty of drama KINGS around.

Women aren't always the hysterical ones. Sometimes men are hysterical. They get mad at anything and everything. When she says yes, he gets mad; and if she says no for the same thing he gets mad. It is always her fault. Being either hysterical or unreasonable is not about Gender. It is about personality, and it makes no difference whether you are a man or a woman. Drama has no Gender.

This woman met a man. They became friends and hung out a few times, but she turned around he was fussing at her about something. She was always doing something wrong. She was not on time. She didn't show up at all. She was too short. She spent too much money on a leather jacket . . . blah, blah, blah. She finally had to tell him, "You do not have the right to fuss at me for any reason you aren't my father! You can express how you feel, but fussing is *not* allowed." The last time he did it, he had cooked and brought her food. As she approached the car to help him with the food, he started fussing at her. She stopped and looked at him and said, "No fussing." He stopped it and hasn't fussed at her since that day.

What to do if your partner is a drama queen:

- Calmly let him know your time is precious, and you would appreciate if he kept the appointment. If he repeats the offense, let him know you cannot go out with him because he is not reliable.
- Show him you mean what you have said. Do not keep repeating yourself. Let him see the action behind your words.
- Stop stressing over the antics of another. Drop him if you need to!

On the other hand, a lot of women don't know when they are being drama queens! They don't think that what they are doing in relationships and on dates is an issue, and then they wonder why they have all these problems! (Ring, Ring! It's for you!) A man can't please a drama queen, and he can't take her anywhere because she finds fault with everything.

Being cool vs. being a drama queen

- Cool people have a real sense of humor. They don't take things too seriously, can easily laugh at themselves and find something fun or humorous in nearly every situation. Drama queens take everything seriously and everything personally. If his coffee order is wrong, he feels personally attacked.

- Cool people have their own happy and fulfilling lives so they don't need someone to entertain them all the time and don't feel bummed out if their partner isn't spending all of his time with them. Drama queens need a someone in their lives in order to feel happy and will get into a relationship with the wrong individuals to avoid being alone and then criticize them for not measuring up to their expectations or constantly break up with them when frustrated.
- Cool people don't complain -- either they look on the bright side of the situation, look for a solution to it, or ask their significant others for an opinion on how to solve something. Drama queens complain about everything, especially things that can't be solved. They'll complain about noisy neighbors, not having enough closet space and a messy roommate, but they'll refuse to move.
- Cool girls are cool with guy time and understand that men need to hang and be guys, just like girls need to chill out or talk on the phone with girlfriends. In fact, cool girls intuitively understand that having some time apart from our guys is necessary so we don't lose ourselves in the relationship. When a drama queen manages to get a boyfriend, she expects him to spend all of his free time with her and she pouts, complains or makes a big deal out of it if he doesn't. She makes a fuss if he wants to spend some time with the guys, because she ditches her friends and former activities to be with him and expects him to do the same.
- Cool people don't try to control partners or rescue them. They let their partners do their own things and learn from their mistakes. They don't try to control all of the situations they are in or make everyone do what THEY think they should do. They go with the flow and let everyone follow their own paths. Drama queens are control freaks and rescuers. They don't trust

or believe their partners can function without their input. They tell their partners what to wear, what to eat and when to take a nap, ad nauseam. They treat them like children. They try to control every situation and make a stink if something doesn't go their way.

- Cool don't "people-please" partners or do things to try to get them to like them more or to spend more time with them. They set boundaries with their time and energy and know that if they have to jump through hoops for a person, that person is not the right one for them. Drama queens "people-please" partners and bend over backwards doing nice things to try to get them to like them more or to spend more time with them. They don't know how to say no so they don't set any boundaries with their time and energy and therefore, they get taken advantage of by others.
- Cool people know how to ask for what they need in a non-demanding way. Drama queens make demands when they want something and whine, cajole and manipulate when their significant other can't or won't meet those demands.
- Cool girls don't try to get validation from men - they have internal validation and know that whatever ideas or feelings they have are okay just as they are. Drama queens are constantly looking for validation from men - they dress provocatively or flirt sexually to get attention (the WRONG attention) from men, they ask their boyfriends questions that put them between a rock and a hard place, questions like "Do these jeans make me look fat?" (NO man wants to answer e that.) They brag about themselves or fish for compliments.
- Cool people are authentic, honest, loyal and forthright. They don't play games, don't lead anyone on when they're not interested, don't hide information, don't cheat, and don't cause drama. Drama queens are fake, lie by omission, and manipulate to get what they want. They don't always know when they're playing games, but they'll lead their partners on when they're not interested because they are worried about hurting egos.

They'll hide information about themselves to sound more appealing. They don't respect themselves or their partner so they allow themselves to get into situations where the temptation is there to cheat, and basically cause drama.
- Cool people know that if they are secure in who they are and treat themselves as valuable treasures, their partner will feel and treat them the same way. Drama queens are insecure and clingy - if they go to a party with their partner, they stick to him like glue all night.

Men don't listen because women nag.
Women nag because men don't listen.

You often hear a wife complain, "My husband never listens to me." Or a husband agonizes, "My wife always nags."

A woman once was ranting about how she'd been talking about wedding arrangements with her fiancé for months, and yet when she asked him a few questions about some detail she'd told him about earlier, he hadn't a clue what she was talking about, not a clue! It left her wondering whether he had heard anything she had *ever* told him.

A common question among women is, "Do men ever listen?" This causes them to repeat and repeat things, and this is perceived as nagging. After the repeated diatribe, the men woefully ask "Do women ever stop nagging?"

If you want your man to listen to you:

- Keep it short. Don't meander on about every little insignificant thing, especially if you've noticed that he has no use for such frivolous details.
- If you have to go into detail, make it interesting. Hold him rapt with a cute anecdote or a funny story that will grab his attention and hold him captive.

- Keep pausing at suitable intervals just to ensure you have his attention. Avoid monologues and give him a chance to have his say too. Actively seek his opinion and ask him for relevant feedback, so that you know he's not just physically present while his mind is elsewhere.
- Stop being predictable and nagging him about the same stuff. If he hasn't gotten the message by now, it's time to change your stance or to get him to move his butt by trying something new.
- Don't even try talking to him when he's in front of the television set. Eliminate all distractions, or wait till he's done with his television or newspaper until you start having your say.
- When you're talking, try and get him to maintain eye contact with you. That way, if his mind wanders, you'll know it by the glazed look in his eyes, unless of course he's perfected the art of appearing that he's listening to you with rapt attention, while he's actually miles away.
- And if you want him to listen and follow through on some instructions, don't order him round. Ask him nicely, check to see if he's comprehended what you've told him, and then act as if the ultimate decision rests with him.

Giving "Birth" is totally different than giving "Life"

Sharing DNA does not make you a parent. It takes a lot more. Providing love, safety nurturing a healthy life style, teaching ethics, morals and nonviolence do." Being a parent is one of the most fulfilling experiences a person can have. There is a natural instinct that seems to come to a new parent, but there are also bits of advice that can help when you are challenged in the growing up years. The most important thing, however, that any parent can give their child, is a sense of being loved; and the most important thing that any parent can remember is that they don't have to be infallible to be a "perfect" parent.

Being a good parent is a challenge, but here are some tips to help you provide a great foundation in your relationship with your kids.

Express love and affection.

A gentle cuddle, a little encouragement, appreciation, approval or even a smile can go a long way to boost the confidence and well-being of your children. Sadly, many children seek this kind of acceptance from their peers (who are wholly unqualified). Give lots of hugs and some kisses. Love them unconditionally. Don't force them to be who you think they should be in order to earn your love. Let them know that you will always love them no matter what.

Listen to them.

The only way children learn how to handle the real world is by positive interaction with their parents. Too many parents think they have to do everything for their kids, creating dysfunctional adults, and then they wonder why they never leave home. Now, if you listen and work with your kids, they can learn the way of the world safely. Express interest in your children and involve yourself in their lives. Create an atmosphere in which they can come to you with any problem, however large or however small.

Respect your children and they will respect you.

Respect their privacy as you would want them to respect yours. For example, if you teach your child that your room is out of boundaries to them, respect the same with their room. Allow them to feel that once they enter their room(s) they can know that no one will look through their drawers, or read their diary.

Teach them what is right and wrong. If you are religious, take them to the religious institute you follow. If you are agnostic, teach them your moral stance on things. In either case, don't be hypocritical or be prepared for your child to point out that you are not "practicing what you preach."

Don't argue with your spouse in front of the children.

If they are sleeping, argue quietly. Modern divorce rates have children feeling insecure and fearful when they hear parents bickering. In addition, children will learn to argue with each other the same way they hear their parents argue with each other. Show them that when people disagree, they can discuss their differences peacefully.

Do not force them by beating or hurting them.

It will only cause resentment and make them go against you. Also, you will get arrested, and your child will be placed in foster care. If you have multiple children, they may be separated.

Take an interest in your child's interests.

If your son likes music, buy him a guitar and watch him play. Ask questions, like what is your favorite type of music, what is your favorite song, etc. If your daughter is interested in fashion, take her out for a shopping spree. Ask her what her favorite thing about fashion is. Don't be afraid to ask, just don't be pushy. Also, when you call out for your child and they say," What?" in a loud, angry voice, tell them to never mind; and talk to them when they don't seem so upset. Sometimes when they yell in that kind of voice you should ask them what's wrong. If they say nothing is wrong that means you need to go in there to find out what's wrong. Sometimes let them come to you.

> ***Maybe you gave me birth, but that doesn't mean you have the right to run my whole life.***

Finders Keepers Losers Weepers

Some parents make a big mistake when they think they have the right to make decisions for their children and when they think, "I'm your parent, so I know better than you." Maybe you are a parent, but that doesn't mean you can't allow them to experience life for themselves - just don't just lose total control. If you make decisions for them all the time, they won't learn how to live with the consequences resulting from the choices they make. Since they will have to learn to think for themselves sometime, it's best if they start when you are there to help minimize negative consequences and accentuate positive consequences. Children need to learn that their own actions have consequences (good and bad). By doing so, it helps them to become good decision makers and problem solvers so that they are prepared for independence and adulthood. This doesnot mean you set no rules or boundaries. Do not miss this crucial step. You must explain their options, and the consequences of each option, and then live with whatever options they select. Teach them right from wrong when they are young, and they will (more often than not) be able to make their own decisions, instead of listening to others.

Remember your child is not an extension of you. Your child is an individual under your care, not a chance for you to relive your life through them. If your daughter doesn't want to study medicine and become a doctor don't get angry. This is your child's life and she can make her own decisions about her life vocation. Understand it's okay if your child thinks differently from you. Don't get mad because they have a different opinion. Don't laugh at them, or their friends. Who cares if your daughter listens to hip hop music and wears too much eyeliner? She's still your daughter. You might not do what your kids do, but that is their decision, not yours. You have a big impact on their lives already. You choose what school they go to, what they eat for dinner and the amount of allowance they get, among many other things.

Many children are victims to the unfulfilled goals of their parents.*ns.

Finders Keepers Losers Weepers

Some parents never fulfilled their own childhood dreams and blame their parents for not giving them the chance to do it. They try to give chances they didn't have to their children. Unfortunately, they sometimes forget to let their children choose what they want to do. Although it is difficult, the best thing we can give our children is independence. We need to raise our children to think for themselves, make their own decisions and to live with the consequences of those decisions. We cannot force them to be something we want them to be. We must let them be what they want to be.

Before you say your son is ungrateful, ask what kind of a father you have been.

Do not blame your children if they throw you in the streets when you old. It is probably you who undervalued your family, encouraged individualism and self-loving. When a mother or father tells a child to leave the family, because the child has reached the age of majority, or is impatient for the child to get out, get a job and rent an apartment, and move away, and then the child makes no attempt to keep in contact with you, what can you expect?

Not everyone who is a parent understands the meaning of the word, *family.* Most couples get married for personal reasons such as love or needing a life partner. For them, having kids is the next move. Having a family and NOT being a family, they think they just have to take care of their kids until they become independent and leave. In some cultures they even treat them as investments. When there are no true family bonds, the struggle in those "families" is obvious. These families are shattered, they suffer and are disconnected to one another, are not involved with each other's lives, have no communication, fight, hate, and reject one another.

Parents need to make real bonds with their kids from day one, being literally involved with their lives. Guiding, protecting, making them feel like they belong, and at the same time teaching them to be independents, is the way you grow together as a family. Teach values and be their role models. Show love through acts of tenderness, devotion, sharing, and embracing. And when you give them all these things make your kids realize that they're loved and accepted no matter what, even when they start their own lives later, then they can't leave you and you won't send them away. They'll be around because they live you, not because they feel any obligations or duties, but simply because they need to be home with their beloved precious parents.

Being a step-parent is difficult.

She said "I have step-parents on both sides and I when my mum first got together with my step-dad, I was a bitch. Now I've grown up a lot more (they've been together for three years), and I can see how he cares for me like my Dad does and would always look out for me. My step-mum is much the same. Sometimes I can see how much he wishes that he was our dad rather than our step-dad."

Parenting isn't easy, but it's very rewarding in so many ways!

This phrase was put on a public website to find out how people thought about it. The sampling was 630 adults and 84% of these adults agreed with the above phrase.

Being a stepchild is pretty tough as well. I've known a few people in my life who seem slack (at best) about introducing new 'daddies' to their kids, and the poor kids are a mess; but the parent is too wrapped up in the new relationship to notice.

When two people get married, they expect to stay together forever; but sometimes people's feelings change over time, even when they have children together they both love. A couple might realize they would be happier apart than together, and so they choose to get divorced. This is never an easy decision.

Sometimes a spouse dies and the husband or wife is forced to start over. Despite all the pain of losing someone they love, in time they might find someone with whom they want to share their lives again.

When either of these things happen, then another whole family is created. A new husband or wife for your parent means a new stepparent for you. It's normal to be sad and scared as your family changes. and it may take some time to get adjusted to your new family situation.

If we treat our step children with commitment to the spouse instead of personal feelings that vary, we then would always be able to love equally.

You can't stop wishing that things were the way they were.

Someone else is watching TV in the living room when there's a show on that you wanted to watch, or someone is taking extra-long showers in the bathroom. . . It's not easy sharing your parent and your home with a stepparent. (It can be even harder if your stepparent has children, and you have stepsiblings.) Don't be afraid to let your mom or dad know you miss spending time them alone.

Love is a feeling, especially UNCONDITIONAL love.

You can show your stepchildren love without having to "love" them as much as your own children. Also, if you refer to step children as "baggage" you are judgmental and trying to make step parents feel bad when they have nothing to feel bad about and are obviously trying their best.

Love takes time to develop.

Finders Keepers Losers Weepers

Loving your stepchild can be both simple and hard. It is not enough for parents, stepparents and extended family to feel a deep glow of love for the children in your circle of influence. You must convey that feeling into a message that is heard, felt and integrated by the child. Children need to be told both verbally and non-verbally how much they are valued for just being them. You have not experienced the effects of living and caring for this child as your spouse has. Your attachment must grow naturally and without undue pressure if you are to experience the affection for your stepchild that you desire.

Protect your relationship.

The best predictors for stepfamily development are a strong couples' relationship and a positive stepparent-stepchild relationship. An attempt to force love will likely only lead to resentment and a negative relationship with your stepchild, as well as spousal discord.

Don't make it or take it personally.

All families have squabbles, and all children say they wish their parents and caregivers were more lenient, generous or understanding. We all try to do the best we can with what we have been given, but we are the adults and must make sure that no matter what the children have given or called us, that we give them guidance, love, discipline and respect. It is our obligation to set consistent boundaries and to assist them in growing into self-directed, contributing members of society.

Make room for grieving and loving.

Freedom of emotional expression is the key to the potential for true love to develop in family relationships. A forced approach will only lend itself towards tensions that disrupt rather than cement your new family bonds. Keep in mind the saying made popular in the '70's: You cannot push a river, it flows by itself!

Start and end each day on a positive note.

Remember to use body language to indicate approval. A hug, high five, pat on the back or smile says so much without saying anything verbal. It has been said that the eyes are the windows of our souls. If that is indeed true, and I think it is, make sure your eyes always say "I'm glad to see you and I am glad you are in my life." Recognize when your child is helpful and cooperative. Many times we take it for granted when our children do their chores without being reminded and are pleasant to the family and write down messages. We only react, sometimes loudly and with negative body language, when the message wasn't given, the chore wasn't done quickly enough or the attitude is less than approachable.

Have family meetings.

It is good to remember a family is an organization. In fact, it is the basic organization of society. This is just one of the reasons I am such a proponent of family meetings. You wouldn't think of running a successful business without a plan, goal setting meetings, team building sessions and clear missions and expectations. Why not explore the value of family meetings?

Truly listen to them.

One of the most effective ways to show a child you love them to pay attention when they are talking. Be empathic while accepting your child's feelings and try to maintain eye contact while they are sharing with you. Children are often deeply upset over things that seem pretty trivial to adults. When we brush off or trivialize their concerns, they think we are rejecting them.

You might surprise yourself when you realize one day that you can't imagine your life without your stepparent anymore.

Finders Keepers Losers Weepers

While the above is quite true, it's also important to understand that when you get along with your stepparent, it does not mean you care less for your parents, especially a parent you may no longer live with most of the time. A caring stepmother understands that you still love your mother and enjoy spending time with her. She will also understand how much you still love your mother your mother has died. Families are about love and understanding, not about competing with each other.

The worst unexpected news for a pregnant woman

If you recently experienced a miscarriage, it's important to find the support you need to get through this difficult time. For most women, the loss of a pregnancy is also the loss of a child-and a dream. The grief that comes afterwards can be riveting, complex, and confusing, to say the least. Many women are shocked at the intensity of their feelings, especially if this is their first miscarriage.

For some women, subsequent pregnancies can bring a sense of hope, for others intense anxiety. You may notice feelings resurfacing near your due date or on subsequent anniversaries of your loss. Again, there is no right or wrong way to treat your feelings. Losing a pregnancy is something that you'll always remember. But when you deal with your feelings in a positive manner and get the support you need, eventually you will feel comfortable bringing joy back into your life.

Miscarriage is a serious issue no matter whether it is attended with grave symptoms or comes with no symptoms. If it occurs shortly after conception, during the first few months of married life, it is serious, if not in its physical consequences, it is in its significance, because it establishes the tendency to miscarry... a tendency that may result in great mental distress because of the worry and fear it engenders.

Realize the following:

1. **What you are feeling is normal:** How can I say that when I don't even know what you are feeling? Well first of all, I do know and it sucks; but secondly, because everyone handles things differently, and that is OK. Commonly, you will have times when you think that you can no longer feel at all and other times when the emotion is so strong that you think that it will overwhelm you. Whatever it is, that is okay. As the days and weeks go by this will lessen, but it may take awhile. Quite often, it can help to talk to a grief counselor (even if you just go with no agenda and let them ask questions and direct the process). Many people feel "broken," and that is fine too. Most likely, you will not feel like yourself for quite awhile.

2. **You must give yourself and your partner time and understanding:** Just because your spouse does not seem to be handling it the same as you does not have to be a problem. This is just a fact of handling grief. Try to be understanding and remember that there is not one set method that works in all cases. If you can work through it together, then in the long run you can get through this and perhaps even have a better relationship.

3. **Handling pregnancy after miscarriage is largely an emotional struggle:** Parents may be extremely anxious and fearful about experiencing another miscarriage. There are many support groups, books, and therapists available to help cope with fears that arise during pregnancy. Knowing the facts of one's situation and being well-prepared to deal with a miscarriage (should it happen) may also provide some relief. Overall, the best strategy for handling

pregnancy after miscarriage is having a strong network of support with multiple sources of help.

If your spouse isn't able to be as supportive as you need them to be don't be too harsh on them. Talk to a therapist, your priest or rabbi, or even to a close friend. Whatever you do, don't just sit back and wait for someone to ask how you're feeling. Chances are it'll never happen.

When I get married it will be a person I love not a baby machine.

Would you break up with your partner if they couldn't give you a baby? 7985 adults were asked this question. 91% said no, and 9% said yes. Adoption is an answer if you both want kids. Love should not be dependent on your ability to reproduce.

Adoption can be one of the most rewarding experiences of your life. Anyone who plans to adopt must also be prepared to properly deal with the finances, time, and other significant lifestyle commitments that will be necessary for parenting to be a success. Your commitment will be tested during the process, and during parenting years. Before you decide to adopt, be sure you are ready and able to give this child all the love and attention he or she needs and deserves.

Love is not a reward and hate is not a punishment (Conditional love)

The love that depends on what is received from the person the love is given to, the love asks for something in return, is conditional love. True love must be unconditional.

Conditional love sends the following messages:
1. "I have done so much for you, so now you should do this for me."
2. "I need your attention, your sympathy, your consent, your time, your presence, your love."

3. "I want you to live your life according to my beliefs and ideas."
4. "I need you to need me, and to look after me exactly the way I have in mind."
5. "If you don't do what I say, I will fall ill or become very unhappy."

Parents use their love to threaten and control children. Love becomes a weapon when parents make their love and make giving it conditioned on their children's success or failure. You may create subtle conditional love without even realizing it. When your children are successful, it's natural for them to feel happy and excited, and when they do poorly to feel sad and disappointed. Because you experience your children's successes and failures vicariously, you may express these same emotions empathically back to your children without any intention of conveying outcome love. But your children may not yet be sophisticated enough to understand that you are simply sharing their joys and disappointments. Instead, your children see strong positive emotions from you when they succeed and strong negative emotions when they fail. These inadvertent messages create the appearance of outcome love and may produce many of the same difficulties in children as those resulting from parents who actively express conditional love. We need to explain to our children that no matter what they do, we still love them. Love is not a reward. Hate cannot be a punishment.

The Columbia University researchers Melissa Kamins and Carol Dweck discovered that children who believed that their self-worth was dependent on how they performed were highly self-critical, showed strong negative emotions, judged their performances severely, and demonstrated less persistence following setbacks. This research shows that conditional love produces children who live in a constant state of fear. They are maniacally driven to succeed in order to receive their parents' love, yet they have a powerful dread of failure and the anticipated loss of love from their parents.

Finders Keepers Losers Weepers

More than 50 years ago, the psychologist Carl Rogers suggested that simply loving our children wasn't enough. We have to love them unconditionally, he said — for who they are, not for what they do.

Chapter Thirty-Four

Do You Scare Men Away?
Women who scare men away

Do you try to change him?

Do you continue to attempt to alter the way your man dresses, the friends he chooses or the foods he eats. Part of a relationship is fully accepting the other person. Remember, you loved him because he is who he is.

Do you say things are fine when they're not?

Women tend to give an unconvincing "fine," then either act irritated or bring the situation up in an argument down the road. Men are task-oriented, so if you say you are fine, he's moving on with things. When you don't move on as well, it confuses and frustrates him. Good communication is the key to any relationship, so either speak up when you're irked or consider it water under the bridge.

Are you an aggressive woman?

While a lot of men concur that they like a woman to be aggressive and take the initiative in the bedroom, they somehow don't feel the same when women take over in the boardroom. The high-flying career woman pretty often finds it really hard to get a decent date, either because she's so busy with climbing the corporate ladder or because the men find her success too intimidating. Even some of the more successful men prefer a woman who can be there for them, not someone who has her own stress-filled career and can give them a run for their money in the brains department. If he has that attitude, move on and find another man in a different boardroom.

Do you call your mom for everything?

Men understand that moms and daughters are tight, but they like to see that you have a mind of your own. After all, if your man wanted your mom's opinion on things, he'd just date her.

Do you trying to control him?

Trying to control or manipulate his thoughts, beliefs, and actions will result in a failed relationship.

Do you want a commitment more than him?

A man feels the noose tightening around his neck and can't wait to make good his escape. After all she's sounding the death-knell for his freedom. If he isn't on the same wave length, find someone who is.

Do you have a record of dating jerks?

Men don't want women that have excess baggage and emotional problems. A disrupted and badly disjointed family life, and/or psycho ex-boyfriends or husbands breed potential problems. If you are a mess, you need to seek therapy before getting into another serious relationship.

Do You Scare Women Away?

How men scare women away:

1. **Being insincere:** Obviously, women love compliments. But when you throw out too many early on in the relationship or even on the first date, she's just going to think you're insincere.

2. **Being too focused on sex:** She already knows you want to do her. So if you rush things, or guilt-trip her into sex, she's not going to put out, and she'll question your intentions. Women want to be valued for things other than their bodies, and they know solid relationships can't be based on sex alone. Some women really do want to wait for marriage.

3. **Being cheap:** Women are drawn to men who can protect and provide for them. It's fine to go Dutch treat every third or fourth date, but making her pay too early sends the signal that you're not the sort of guy she with whom can have a future.

4. **Talking about ex(s):** No woman wants to hear about your ex. And it doesn't matter whether you're saying good things or bad things. Either way, it shows you have too much baggage.

5. **Being inconsiderate:** A woman appreciates a man by how he communicates with others. Thus, she predicts, how a man will talk to her after closer acquaintance. If you want to impress a woman, show more respect for others. Remember, she is watching you.

6. **Trying to control her:** Do not try to control your woman by telling her when to get online, what picture to send, what questions to answer, and by insisting that she stop talking with other men, control the way she dresses, etc.

7. **He's a Mommy's boy:** Mommy's boy is a term for a man who is excessively attached to his mother at an age when men are expected to be independent (e.g. live on their own, be economically independent). Women don't like a mommy's boy even if they want their sons to be their mommy's boys! A mother-bonded man is seen as one who gives control of his own life to his mother in exchange for a sense of security. If the mother has more than one son, then she will have, at the most, one mother's boy, usually the eldest or youngest son. The relationship between mother and mother's boy is thought to be "symbiotic." The mother enjoys controlling her mother's boy.

How to spot a mommy's boy:

1. **He tells her everything, EVERYTHING:** After a certain age, you stop telling your parents everything. His mother doesn't need to know how much is in your bank account. If she wants to know if the two of you are planning on producing a grandchild, or how much your bartender gig pays, she can ask. You don't have to tell her. And neither does he.

2. **He talks to her every day:** What makes this so frightening is the fact that when anything significant or insignificant happens in his life, the first woman he thinks to call is his mom, not you. It's one thing if your guy talks to his mom once a day because she has no one in the world but him (which is still a scary thought) but if he and his mom have telephone conversations multiple times a day to gossip or just tell each other the little things that girlfriends usually tell one another, head for the hills.

3. **He treats you like a maid:** She's cooked for him, cleaned for him, and made his bed for years. And he loves it. Now you'll

have to do it, because he's incapable of taking care of himself. He's a man-child through and through. You're his wife. Not his mom. He no longer needs the lady of the house cleaning up his crumbs or making him four-course meals after a 10-hour workday

4. **She cleans your house without your permission:** She arrives unannounced with a bucket full of cleaning supplies wearing neon-yellow rubber gloves. She claims she's just here to "tidy up" and your guy treats her like a scrubbing savior.

5. **He compares you to her:** He's beginning to really push the envelope by comparing everything you do or say to the way his mother does it. Of all the signs that he's a mommy's boy, this is one that will wear thin quickly.

6. **She always right:** No matter if she insults you or hurts you, he never says a word in your defense. But if you dared to say anything remotely insulting about his mother in private, like "I can't stand it when your mom belittles me," he immediately jumps to her defense. It seems you just can't win.

7. **He will never STOP:** A boy who loves his mother dearly won't stop because it's hurting you. He'd rather let you go than lose his mother. And before it comes down to an ultimatum that you're going to lose, you should run, not walk, away.

Why women don't like mommy's boys!!

1. **Women don't like to share when it comes to men:** Even if it's with his mother, if a man always puts his mother before his woman, no matter what the occasion, chances are his woman will end up resenting him and leave him. The main reason why women don't like mama's boys is because competing with the woman who gave birth to him just isn't an option. On the flip-

side the evil mother-in-law is an indicator that some women hate competition from other women at all ages. So maybe the term stems from deep-seated insecurity about competing with another woman's agenda.

2. **Guys who are mommy's boys never change:** They just never change, never ever! His mother will think that no other woman will ever be good enough for him. She will not break his heart, but his lover will. His mother is his whole world, so there is no chance to see the other side of the world.

3. **I'm your wife NOT your maid:** Marriage is about sharing. couples share domestic tasks such as laundry, cooking, and cleaning. The problem is that a mama's boy is often used to his mom cooking his meals or doing his laundry for him.

4. **They rarely think they're wrong:** Mama's boys are so used to being treated with unconditional love that they rarely think they're wrong.

5. **I married you NOT your mama:** The fact is that mommy's boys sometimes make the mistake of telling their mothers certain private things. There are some issues you might want to keep between you and your special lady.

My partner is a mommy's boy, how can I deal with Him?

1. **Don't give him an ultimatum:** Accept that your partner's a mommy's boy, and nothing is going to change it. He has been and will continue to be one. Work with the situation instead of against it.

2. **Get to know his Mother:** Make friends with his mother. If his mother loves you, he will love you. Go shopping, go to a movie, ask her for advice, and ask her how she cooks that

dinner. Turn her into an ally, not an enemy. This can be done by chatting when she calls 20 times a day, sending her special cards on holidays and taking time out to spend time with her one on one. Creating a bond with his mother ensures that no one ends up jealous.

3. **Take advantage of the situation:** If your boyfriend is whining about not having clean clothes or a hot dinner, tell him to trek on down to his mom's so she can do a load of laundry and feed him. When he complains about money, likewise send him her way to get some.

4. **"Just you two" activities:** Find some "just you two" activities. If she has a tendency to invite herself along, find an inventive activity that she isn't likely to join in on. Try paintball, ice-fishing, rock-climbing, or any other adventures activity that isn't mom-friendly. Unusual dates will give you and your mama's boy a chance to bond while sending a signal to mom that you need alone time. Remain your own, individual self. You don't need to start acting like his mother or making meatloaf like she does. Retain your own stellar personality that brought you and your boyfriend together in the first place.

5. **Befriend another important family member:** The mom's sister, mother, close family friend or husband may be able to open her eyes to what a great person you really are.

6. **Lastly,** remember majority of the time, men do not realize they are mommy's boys. They are simply used to being a certain way because that's all they have known. The likelihood of them admitting they are one is very slim. Try approaching it this way, and you will more than likely see a better result.

CHAPTER THIRTY-FIVE

Should you get a pet?

A pet can become a part of the family, and to be loved as one

Research shows a link with pets and happiness, and with health too. Pets can lower blood pressure, decrease stress, lower cholesterol levels, even increase survival rates for those with cardiac problems. And of course they're great company.

Many programs now connect people with older pets. Although kittens and puppies are cute, they aren't necessarily a great choice. Not only can adopting a senior animal save its life, the pet may be a better fit. Mature cats and dogs are easier to handle. They usually have calmer temperaments. Many older dogs are already well trained, eliminating the need to spend large amounts of time and patience on things like housebreaking. With a young animal, you often can't tell the pet's size and personality until it is full-grown, so there are fewer unwelcome surprises with a mature pet! These cats and dogs really need a loving home. Some shelters reduce or waive the adoption fee if you adopt an older pet.

Finders Keepers Losers Weepers

Animals give you one thing better than R-E-S-P-E-C-T. They give you unquestioning, unbridled, unwavering love. Did your boyfriend or girlfriend suddenly take the high road or your boss hand you your final pay check? Never fear, Fluffy is near. Treat your pet with the respect it deserves and you will be repaid in kind with lifelong attention and affection, especially when you need it most.

Learning invaluable life skills that enable a person to become a better person is one of the most rewarding things you can do. Learning to share love, provide affection, and give attention to a pet are three qualities that enhance the personal quality of human life. Not convinced? Ask any pet owner about the satisfaction of caring for a pet, and whether they'd do it all over again if they could.

CHAPTER THIRTY-SIX
Pregnant women are attractive.

I have no qualms in saying that pregnant women look extremely wonderful and sexy! It all depends on how you feel about yourself. Pregnancy is a great thing. You live with two souls in the same body. It is not about being pregnant today. It's about being pregnant for nine months!

Most psychologists find that pregnant women tend to fall into two camps: those that love their pregnant bodies and those who simply can't stand them! Many women come to appreciate the curves pregnancy offers them. Voluptuous breasts and a feminine stomach help some women to feel ultra-feminine, strong, and sexual. Other women simply hate the added weight, stretch marks, and big stomach that pregnancy entails. Many women fight with their bodies continuously in order manipulate and control them.

Maybe you've changed a little bit. You've gained about 13 pounds now, maybe more; but feeling the baby move inside you is worth it. Some women almost feel because her hubby will never get to know what it feels like to have someone kicking his bladder from the inside, or punching his ribcage like a tiny boxer.

If you are a pregnant woman you should:

1. **Develop a positive body image during your pregnancy:** Body image during pregnancy is merely a matter of perception. The key is adopting the right perception throughout your pregnancy.

2. **You are carrying the miracle of life within you:** Remember, No matter how much weight you gain, whether you have acne or not and regardless of the stretch marks pregnancy brings, your body is changing in a remarkable way because you are helping nurture and welcome a new life into the world.

3. **Pregnancy weight gain is a normal and natural process:** Your weight gain is as much the result of your increasing metabolism and caloric needs as it is your expanding uterus. As you put on weight you help shield your baby from disease and provide a warm and nurturing home.

When your wife is pregnant you should:

1. **Things to Do For Your Pregnant Wife:** Maybe your wife is the pregnant one here but if she will be a mother it means you will be a father too! It is really great thing will happen in your life; both of you; as she has a role you have a role too.

2. **Stop telling her to rest**: Quit telling her to sit down and rest or take a nap. She has stopped trying to keep the baby in. She is tired of resting and waiting. The best way to get the baby out seems to be moving. Let her move and hope gravity helps speed up the process. Maybe she has a baby but she is not a baby.

3. **Stop telling her she looks tired**: She's pregnant so she's always tired and therefore will always look tired. Reminding

her of this will only remind her that she has a few things to say to you and that scruffy hair growing on your face.

4. **Buy the baby stuff**: Diapers are good. Cute baby pajamas are better. I recommend only getting one thing at a time. Just seeing a cute baby something is enough to get a smile. Would you rather have a smile every couple of days or just once when you buy a whole new wardrobe at one time?

5. **Take care of low stuff**: Pick up stuff off the floor before she gets around to it. Move the laundry so she doesn't have to bend over. Be A Good Mom likes to remind us that she only can bend over a handful of times a day. Don't make her waste those bend over doing chores.

Chapter Thirty-Seven
What is personal success?

Which more defines personal success (A) Career (D) Family? Divorced Successful CEO vs. Unemployed Successful Parent?

This question was asked in a public discussion website, the result was 22% for career and 78% for family and the sample was taken from 220 adults.

I believe family is more important than a career. You can have many careers, but only one family; and you get out of it what you put into it. I think successful family life will lead to other successful things including career, because having a family is motivates success. We are not greater the sum of our histories. We would have no past without the heritage of our family name, no life without their efforts to raise us, and no future without our children. It took millions of people to meet. love, suffer, labor and even die over a millennium of time to create us. The generations before us brought our genetics together at this place and time, so we could have success as unique individuals. Compared to all that effort and care, our own success is pitiful.

But I must admit I was shocked when I saw the result of the above survey, because I thought that nowadays career was much important than family to most people. We live in a world where career defines personal success. But the truth is, when you reach the end of your life your career is obsolete, your legacy is your family. No one is going to remember that you were a workaholic and spent all your time at your job. But your family will remember whether you spent time with them. Having a good career without a family with whom to share your happiness is what I would consider a nightmare.

True love exists when a man looks at his seventy-five year old wife and she looks to him the same as when they first met.

Every time I see older couples walking in street, or going out with each other, I like to watch how they look at one another with loving eyes. That kind of relationship after all those years is not just based on love. It is based on love, friendship, attachment, nearness, cordiality, companionship. . . It is based on everything that has made up their lifetime together. One seventy year old woman described her husband by saying, "He was my lover until I gave birth to my first child. Then he was my older kid. He is my father, my brother, my sister, my mother, my whole world. . . especially after all my sons got married. I know what the meaning of true love is when I look into his eyes."

Even if you're sixty or seventy-five years old, it is never too late to fall madly or gently, or even sacredly, in love, because you can find true love at any time. Or maybe you will fall in love all over again with your spouse. Once a couple gets comfortable in a situation their goals and ideas begin to meld until they no longer know what they really want, but staying in love, true love is not impossible. Love and marriage are lifetime projects, not projects of only the moment. Try something you always thought you'd enjoy, but never really considered doing, such as taking dance classes or learning to ride a horse. Finally, Take the marriage quiz and see how you score.

Marriage Quiz

1. **What is your age?**
   - ☐ Under 18 Years Old
   - ☐ 18 to 24 Years Old
   - ☐ 25 to 30 Years Old
   - ☐ 31 to 40 Years Old
   - ☐ 41 to 50 Years Old
   - ☐ 51 to 60 Years Old
   - ☐ Over 60 Years Old

2. **What is your gender?**
   - ☐ Male
   - ☐ Female

3. **Do you love your partner?**
   - ☐ No
   - ☐ Yes
   - ☐ Sometimes

4. **Do you know your partner's favorite color, meal, dress/waist size?**
   - ☐ No
   - ☐ Yes
   - ☐ Sometimes

Finders Keepers Losers Weepers

5. **Is your partner usually a great help in solving problems?**
   ☐ No
   ☐ Yes
   ☐ Sometimes

6. **Do you enjoy making plans for your future together?**
   ☐ No
   ☐ Yes
   ☐ Sometimes

7. **Can you cheer him up when he's down?**
   ☐ No
   ☐ Yes
   ☐ Sometimes

8. **Do you share common hobbies/pastimes with your partner?**
   ☐ No
   ☐ Yes
   ☐ Sometimes

9. **Do you go out of your way to tell or show your partner how much you love them every day?**
   ☐ No
   ☐ Yes
   ☐ Sometimes

10. **Do you know what your partner likes about work?**

- ☐ No
- ☐ Yes
- ☐ Sometimes

11. Have you similar interests and activities?
- ☐ No
- ☐ Yes
- ☐ Sometimes

12. Do you think your partner is faithful?
- ☐ No
- ☐ Yes
- ☐ Sometimes

13. Can you name your partner's three best friends?
- ☐ No
- ☐ Yes
- ☐ Sometimes

14. Do you know what satisfies your partner emotionally?
- ☐ No
- ☐ Yes
- ☐ Sometimes

15. Has your partner ever hit you or been physical with you?

- No
- Yes
- Sometimes

16. Are you happy in your relationship?

- No
- Yes
- Sometimes

17. Are you able to talk about what is troubling your relationship when tension starts to build between you and your partner?

- No
- Yes
- Sometimes

18. Do you generally feel comfortable with the way anger is expressed in your relationship?

- No
- Yes
- Sometimes

19. Do you generally feel comfortable with the way conflicts and disagreements are handled?

- No

- [ ] Yes
- [ ] Sometimes

20. Are you sexually compatible and comfortable with each other?

- [ ] No
- [ ] Yes
- [ ] Sometimes

21. Are you generally happy with the friends you have in common and how much time you spend socially together?

- [ ] No
- [ ] Yes
- [ ] Sometimes

22. Does your partner introduce you to his/her friends

- [ ] No
- [ ] Yes
- [ ] Sometimes

23. Can you imagine a life without your partner?
- [ ] No
- [ ] Yes
- [ ] Sometimes

Finders Keepers Losers Weepers

24. When you argue does one of you withdraw and not want to talk about it anymore or leaves the scene?
- ☐ No
- ☐ Yes
- ☐ Sometimes

25. Does your partner seem to view your words or actions more negatively than you mean them to be?
- ☐ No
- ☐ Yes
- ☐ Sometimes

26. Does your partner pressure you to do sexual things you don't want to do?
- ☐ No
- ☐ Yes
- ☐ Sometimes

27. Has your partner threatened to hurt you or has he hurt you?
- ☐ No
- ☐ Yes
- ☐ Sometimes

- Did you answer **"Yes"** to questions **from 3 to 22?** If so, you are probably in a pretty comfortable relationship.

- If you answered **"Yes"** or "Sometimes" to questions **from 23 to 27** you may be in an uncomfortable or even dangerous relationship.

How did you score?